‍ W9-BLP-885

At Issue

Nuclear Weapons

Other Books in the At Issue Series:

At Issue

Nuclear Weapons

Louise I. Gerdes, Book Editor

GREENHAVEN PRESS
A part of Gale, Cengage Learning

GALE
CENGAGE Learning

Detroit • New York • San Francisco • New Haven, Conn • Waterville, Maine • London

Christine Nasso, *Publisher*
Elizabeth Des Chenes, *Managing Editor*

For more information, contact:
Greenhaven Press
27500 Drake Rd.
Farmington Hills, MI 48331-3535
Or you can visit our Internet site at gale.cengage.com

Articles in Greenhaven Press anthologies are often edited for length to meet page requirements. In addition, original titles of these works are changed to clearly present the main thesis and to explicitly indicate the author's opinion. Every effort is made to ensure that Greenhaven Press accurately reflects the original intent of the authors. Every effort has been made to trace the owners of copyrighted material.

Cover photograph © Images.com/Corbis.

LIBRARY OF CONGRESS CATALOGING-IN-PUBLICATION DATA

Nuclear Weapons / Louise I. Gerdes, book editor.
p. cm. -- (At issue)
Includes bibliographical references and index.
ISBN 978-0-7377-4308-1 (hardcover)
ISBN 978-0-7377-4307-4 (pbk.)
1. Nuclear nonproliferation--Juvenile literature. 2. Nuclear nonproliferation--Government policy--United States--Juvenile literature. 3. Nuclear arms control--Government policy--United States--Juvenile literature. 4. Nuclear nonproliferation--Iran--Juvenile literature. 5. Nuclear arms control--Iran--Juvenile literature. 6. Nuclear nonproliferation--North Korea--Juvenile literature. 7. Nuclear arms control--North Korea--Juvenile literature. 8. Nuclear nonproliferation--Pakistan--Juvenile literature. 9. Nuclear arms control--Pakistan--Juvenile literature. I. Gerdes, Louise I., 1953-
JZ5675.N856 2009
327.1'747--dc22
2009003286

Printed in the United States of America
2 3 4 5 6   13 12 11 10 09

ED231

Contents

Introduction

In January 2004, Abdul Qadeer (A.Q.) Khan, father of Pakistan's nuclear bomb, confessed to having sold nuclear weapons technology to Iran, North Korea, and Libya. Some speculate that he may have sold this technology to other rogue states and even to terrorists. Khan's shocking confession signaled that a new era of the nuclear age had begun. For many, his revelation shattered any remaining illusion that more than 60 years of nonproliferation efforts would protect the world from nuclear catastrophe. The destructive power of terrorism became vividly clear in the United States following the terrorist attacks of September 11, 2001. Khan's exposure of a nuclear black market intensified concerns that terrorists might be able obtain nuclear technology. According to former Assistant Secretary of Defense Graham Allison, "A nuclear 9/11 in Washington or New York would change American history in ways that [the original] 9/11 didn't." Indeed, he maintains, "It would be as big a leap beyond 9/11 as 9/11 itself was beyond the pre-attack illusion that we were invulnerable." On February 11, 2004, President George W. Bush responded to Khan's startling confession with a seven-point plan to strengthen nonproliferation programs. While many experts applauded his efforts, nonproliferation proposals to keep nuclear weapons out of the hands of terrorists, they claim, face serious challenges. The debate over the effectiveness of nonproliferation strategies is, in many ways, reflective of the overarching nuclear weapons debate.

Nonproliferation efforts began almost as soon as the nuclear genie was out of the bottle. On August 6, 1945, the United States detonated an atomic bomb over Hiroshima, Japan, and another on Nagasaki three days later. These two bombs, which were significantly less destructive than many of the nuclear weapons of today, killed more than 250,000 people.

Japan surrendered shortly thereafter, ending World War II. By 1964, Britain, China, France, and the Soviet Union had joined the nuclear club. These five nuclear powers feared that a nuclear attack by one superpower would inevitably lead to a nuclear response, resulting in global nuclear annihilation. Based on this grim realization, in 1968 the five nations with nuclear weapons agreed to help nonnuclear nations develop nuclear power for peaceful purposes in exchange for the promise that these nations would not develop nuclear weapons. Compliance with this Nonproliferation Treaty (NPT) was to be monitored by the International Atomic Energy Agency (IAEA), created in 1957 to promote the peaceful use of nuclear energy.

Several nations, including India, Israel, and Pakistan, refused to sign the treaty. All have since developed nuclear weapons. Moreover, several signatories have renounced the NPT either openly or by secretly pursuing nuclear weapons. The 1991 Persian Gulf War against Iraq, for example, revealed that Iraqi President Saddam Hussein was trying to develop nuclear weapons. North Korea had also signed the treaty but later renounced it and on October 9, 2006, tested a nuclear weapon. In recent years, another NPT signatory, Iran, is believed by some to be pursuing nuclear weapons. These realities have led some experts to argue that the treaty's weaknesses doom it to failure. "Arms-control regimes are not capable of dealing with the hard cases," claims defense policy expert John Pike. "The logic of the NPT just doesn't get you very far in Tehran [Iran] or Pyongyang [North Korea]," he reasons.

Some commentators claim, however, that proposals to strengthen the NPT can effectively promote nonproliferation. Bush proclaimed in his February 11, 2004, speech, "We're determined to confront [nuclear] threats at the source. We will stop these weapons from being acquired or built. We'll block them from being transferred. We'll prevent them from ever being used. . . . We've shown that proliferators can be discovered and can be stopped." Bush's nonproliferation proposals include, for example, a UN Security Council resolution to criminalize the sale of components that could be used to make nuclear weapons. In addition, he proposed that only Additional Protocol signatories be allowed to import materials and equipment for civilian nuclear reactors. The Additional Protocol of the NPT added teeth to IAEA efforts to monitor nuclear programs by creating a quantitative system to account for nuclear materials and by expanding the IAEA's ability to check for clandestine nuclear facilities. It gave the IAEA the authority to visit any facility, declared or not, to investigate inconsistencies in a state's nuclear declarations. Those who support nonproliferation proposals believe that these strategies will be adequate to deter nuclear proliferation.

Critics claim that these efforts to keep nuclear weapons out of the hands of terrorists face several challenges. One such challenge is inadequate funding. "The Khan network underscores the fact that we're in a race to tighten down security around [nuclear weapons technology] so the terrorists can't get it," argues Wade Boese, research director of the Arms Control Association. "If this is such an urgent priority, which it is, why not fund it like it is and recognize that we're in a race with the terrorists?" Like-minded commentators contend that the $1 billion promised by the United States to support the 1993 Cooperative Threat Reduction (CTR) program is woefully inadequate. The CTR was designed to help Soviet satellite countries destroy nuclear, chemical, and biological weapons. According to nuclear-terrorism expert Matthew Bunn, $1 billion amounts to less than 1 percent of the Defense Department's budget, which in 2004 was $401 billion. Bunn is amazed that despite increasing terrorist threats, funding for CTR programs has not noticeably increased since the September 11, 2001, terrorist attacks.

Another challenge that nonproliferation critics argue must be addressed is identifying which threats pose the greatest risk. Opponents of the invasion of Iraq claim that the war has been a poor use of resources. Some would place Russia's nuclear weapons and materials, which they claim are extremely vulnerable to theft, higher on the list of priorities. Charles B. Curtis, president of the Nuclear Threat Initiative, maintains, "We've still got 120 metric tons of highly enriched uranium and plutonium in Russia alone that we haven't even begun security upgrades on." Another priority threat, in the eyes of some analysts, is Pakistan. Because it is not an NPT signatory, its nuclear-weapons inventory is unknown, as is the extent of Khan's customers. Nevertheless, the known extent of his network shocked even veteran observers. "While there had been suggestions that the Pakistanis were nefariously engaged in both Iran and North Korea," Curtis contends, "the extent of the engagement in Libya and indications that there was an attempt to market proliferation technology in Syria exceeded the darkest suspicions of the intelligence community." The focus on Iraq, detractors declare, proved to be misplaced. "A coherent strategy has got to deal with the most urgent potential sources of supply to terrorists first," defense expert Allison asserts.

Still another challenge to nonproliferation efforts is the United States' mixed record on safeguarding its own nuclear materials. "President Bush's speech was a series of measures that would constrain everybody else," argues nuclear-terrorism expert Bunn. "There was no mention of anything that would constrain the United States," he asserts. In fact, the United States has for years been exporting highly enriched uranium to forty-three countries to help these nations acquire nuclear technology for peaceful purposes. This uranium was supposed to be returned in its original form or as spent fuel. The Energy Department reports, however, that little of the uranium has been recovered. According to the report, there is enough unaccounted for uranium to make approximately 1,000 nuclear weapons. "While we should be locking up materials at risk wherever we can and recovering them when needed, the Department of Energy has been leisurely pursing its program to recover highly enriched uranium at risk in research facilities around the world," contends Curtis. "This is a leisure that we can ill afford," he concludes.

Whether efforts to strengthen the NPT and the IAEA will be adequate to keep nuclear weapons out of the hands of terrorists remains hotly contested. The authors of the viewpoints in *At Issue: Nuclear Weapons* debate the threat of nuclear terrorism as well as other nuclear threats and the challenges and complexities of containing these threats. The significance of the nuclear debate President Bush made clear in his speech at National Defense University. "The way ahead is not easy, but it is clear. We will proceed as if the lives of our citizens depend on our vigilance, because they do."

1

The Proliferation of Nuclear Weapons Is a Serious Problem

Conn Hallinan

Conn Hallinan is a foreign policy analyst for Foreign Policy in Focus, *a publication of the Institute for Policy Studies, a progressive Washington, DC, think tank. Hallinan is also a lecturer in journalism at the University of California, Santa Cruz.*

Modern nuclear weapons have a tremendous capacity for destruction. By signing the Nuclear Nonproliferation Treaty (NPT), the Big Five nuclear powers—the United States, Britain, France, China, and the former Soviet Union—agreed to dismantle their nuclear arsenals in exchange for the promise that other signatory nations would not acquire nuclear weapons. However, the threat posed by nuclear proliferation does not come from nations hoping to acquire them. The danger comes from the Big Five. The United States, for example, has eroded the goal of nonproliferation by its efforts to circumvent nonproliferation treaties. By failing to abide by these treaties, the Big Five encourage other nations to pursue nuclear weapons.

> "Each of the Parties to the Treaty undertakes to pursue negotiations in good faith on effective measures relating to cessation of the nuclear arms race at an early date and to nuclear disarmament, and a Treaty on general and complete disarmament under strict and effective international control."
>
> *Article VI,*
> *Treaty on the Non-Proliferation of Nuclear Weapons, 1968*

"The United States will not use nuclear weapons against any non-nuclear weapon party state to the Non-Proliferation Treaty . . . except in the case of an attack on the United States, its territories or armed forces, or its allies, by such a state allied to a nuclear weapon state. . . ."

Addendum to the Treaty on the Non-Proliferation of Nuclear Weapons, 1978, agreed to by the United Kingdom, the Soviet Union, and endorsed by France. Reaffirmed in 1980 and 1995.

"The leaders of states who use terrorist means against us, as well as those who would consider using, in one way or another, weapons of mass destruction, must understand that they would lay themselves open to a firm and adapted response on our part. This response could be a conventional one. It could be of a different kind."

French President Jacques Chirac visiting the nuclear submarine Vigilant, Jan. 19, 2006.

Treaties are rarely scintillating, but the [40]-year-old Nuclear Non-Proliferation Treaty (NPT) has a certain sparseness of language and precision of meaning that makes it an engaging read. Boiled down, it commits the 177 non-nuclear nations that signed it not to acquire nuclear weapons and the Big Five nuclear powers—the United States, Britain, France, China, and the USSR—to dismantle theirs.

The theory behind it was simple: non-nuclear weapons states would forgo developing nukes on the conditions that, 1) they are never blackmailed with nuclear weapons, and 2) the Big Five get rid of their arsenals.

All of this seems to have gotten lost in the recent uproar over Iran. While Tehran is being accused of trying to scam the NPT by secretly developing nuclear weapons, the open [flouting] of the Treaty by the major nuclear powers is simply ignored.

For almost [40] years the vast majority of the world's nations have adhered to the NPT. Only India, Pakistan, Israel, and possibly North Korea have joined the Big Five, although, at the time the Treaty was signed, a dozen more were on the verge of developing nuclear weapons. In short, the vast bulk of the signers have held to what they agreed to.

The [nuclear] fireball that consumed Hiroshima . . . killed 100,000 people in a single blow. Another 100,000 plus would follow in the months ahead.

Ignoring Treaty Obligations

The Big Five, however, have ignored the obligation to dismantle their nuclear arsenals or to even discuss general disarmament. At the NPT Review Conference [May 2005] the issue did not even come up, a shortcoming which UN General Secretary Kofi Annan called a "disgrace."

Not only have the Big Five refused to consider eliminating their nuclear arsenals, in 2002 the [George W.] Bush Administration's Nuclear Posture Review (NPR) unilaterally overturned the 1978 pledge, and the White House threatened to use nukes on Syria, Iran, and Iraq, all non-nuclear states. The Administration's rationale is that the NPT is not just about nuclear weapons, but "weapons of mass destruction," which it argues, includes chemical and biological weapons. It is a re-interpretation the French appear to embrace as well.

But chemical and biological weapons were specifically excluded from the NPT for the very good reason that they are not weapons of mass destruction.

Chemical weapons are certainly nasty, but generals in World War I found them more an annoyance than a serious threat. While artillery (the big killer), machine guns, and rifles inflicted 8.5 million deaths from 1914–1918, gas [killed only] about 100,000. Chemicals are simply too difficult to deliver and too volatile to do much damage.

Bacteriological warfare is spooky, but even more difficult to make effective. Anthrax may have shut down Washington, but it [killed only] five people.

According to the International Atomic Energy Agency (IAEA), there are presently about 27,000 [nuclear] warheads in the world, many of them capable of being launched with a half hour.

The Capacity for Nuclear Destruction

Nuclear weapons are quite another matter, although as memories of World War II grow dim, it is easy to fall into the equivalence trap.

A brief reminder: The fireball that consumed Hiroshima reached 18 million degrees in one millionth of a second. It evaporated 68% of the city, demolishing structures built to withstand an 8.5 earthquake. It charred trees five miles from ground zero, blew out windows 17 miles from the city's center, and killed 100,000 people in a single blow. Another 100,000 plus would follow in the months ahead.

The bomb that flattened Hiroshima was 15 kilotons. The standard warhead in the U.S. arsenal today—the W-76—is 100 kilotons. A substantial number of our weapons are 250 kilotons, and they range as high as five megatons. One of the latter can eliminate a small country.

According to the International Atomic Energy Agency (IAEA), there are presently about 27,000 such warheads in the world, many of them capable of being launched within a half hour. In accepting the 2005 Nobel Peace Prize, Mohamed El-Baradei, head of the IAEA, said, "More than 15 years after the Cold War, it is incomprehensible to many that the major nuclear weapons states operate with their weapons on hair-trigger alert."

This is the price the world is paying for not insisting that the Big Five do what they agreed to do. And the danger is getting worse. Not from countries like Iran, but from the nuclear weapons establishment—particularly in the United States—that is systematically trying to dismantle the fragile barrier of treaties that hold the beast in check.

The Test-Ban Treaty

One of the key threads in this increasingly tattered web is the 1996 Comprehensive Test Ban Treaty (CTBT). The theory behind the CTBT was that banning tests would prevent any further developments in nuclear weapons technology, particularly the miniaturization of warheads. It was also assumed that no one would risk deploying a weapon which had not been tested. Nuclear devices are tricky and a substantial number of designs produce duds.

A side benefit to the CTBT was that it would also prevent the nuclear powers from randomly pulling warheads off line and testing them to make sure they still worked. The Treaty designers hoped that a lack of confidence in a weapon's reliability was all to the good. If you are not sure something will work, you may be more reluctant to use it.

The major danger in the world today comes . . . from the unwillingness of the major nuclear powers to live up to the promise they made back in 1968.

But the ink was hardly dry when the United States—and, it would appear, France—figured out how to redesign weapons without actually setting them off. Using sophisticated computers, weapon labs in France, and at Livermore, Los Alamos, and Sandia in the United States, began to configure a new generation of nuclear weapons.

Indeed, India pointed to this computer-based U.S. weapons program as one of the reasons why it initiated a round of nuclear tests in 1998, although New Delhi's accusations received virtually no ink in the States.

Violating the Treaty's Spirit

[In 2005] Congress launched the Reliable Warhead Replacement (RWR) program purportedly to insure that the U.S. nuclear arsenal would continue to work. One could certainly make an argument that RWR was a violation of the spirit, if not the letter, of the CTBT.

But according to the local anti-nuclear group Tri-Valley CARE, the program is also retooling warheads to make them smaller in yield (and therefore more likely to be used), capable of taking out deeply buried targets, and able to destroy chemical and biological weapons.

This redesign effort was revealed in a report by William Schneider Jr., chair of the Defense Science Board, who wrote in 2004 that the United States must not just simply improve nuclear weapons capacity "on the margins," but must develop "weapons more relevant to the future threat environment."

It is possible the United States could accomplish this without resuming testing (although [former] Secretary of Defense Donald Rumsfeld has openly talked about violating the test ban). But even if the United States doesn't test, other nations will certainly not allow themselves to fall behind just because they don't have fancy computers. If the United States continues on this path, other nations will resume testing, which will, in turn, encourage non-nuclear nations to begin their own programs. It is estimated that up to 40 nations could manufacture nuclear weapons.

"The most important thing," ElBaradei told the *Financial Times*, "is to make the big boys understand that the major league is not an exclusive club. If you are not going to dissolve that club, others are going to join it. A world of haves and have-nots is not sustainable."

The major danger in the world today comes not from countries like Iran and North Korea, but from the unwillingness of the major nuclear powers to live up to the promise they made back in 1968. "The central problem in halting nuclear proliferation," says Selig Harrison, director of the Asia Program of the Center for International Policy and a former India bureau chief for the *Washington Post*, "lies in the failure of the original nuclear powers that signed the NPT to live up to Article 6, in which they pledged to phase out their nuclear weapons."

2

The United States Can Manage a Nuclear Iran

Barry R. Posen

Barry R. Posen is a professor of political science at the Massachusetts Institute of Technology and author of Inadvertent Escalation: Conventional War and Nuclear Risks.

Fears of a nuclear Iran are overstated. The U.S. nuclear deterrent, along with domestic reforms and improved intelligence operations in the region, are adequate to manage a nuclear Iran. If Iran were to sell nuclear weapons to terrorists, for example, it would risk becoming a nuclear target itself. Moreover, the consequences of gambling that the United States will not protect its Middle Eastern allies against Iranian nuclear blackmail or aggression are too great. If Iran even appears to be readying nuclear weapons for attack against its neighbors, the United States might launch a pre-emptive nuclear strike.

The intense concern about Iran's nuclear energy program reflects the judgment that, should it turn to the production of weapons, an Iran with nuclear arms would gravely endanger the United States and the world. An Iranian nuclear arsenal, policymakers fear, could touch off a regional arms race while emboldening Tehran to undertake aggressive, even reckless, actions.

But these outcomes are not inevitable, nor are they beyond the capacity of the United States and its allies to defuse.

Indeed, while it's seldom a positive thing when a new nuclear power emerges, there is reason to believe that we could readily manage a nuclear Iran.

Defusing a Middle Eastern Arms Race

A Middle Eastern arms race is a frightening thought, but it is improbable. If Iran acquires nuclear weapons, among its neighbors, only Israel, Egypt, Saudi Arabia and Turkey could conceivably muster the resources to follow suit.

Israel is already a nuclear power. Iranian weapons might coax the Israelis to go public with their arsenal and to draw up plans for the use of such weapons in the event of an Iranian military threat. And if Israel disclosed its nuclear status, Egypt might find it diplomatically difficult to forswear acquiring nuclear weapons, too. But Cairo depends on foreign assistance, which would make Egypt vulnerable to the enormous international pressure it would most likely face to refrain from joining an arms race.

If a terrorist group used one of Iran's nuclear weapons, Iran would have to worry that the victim would discover the weapon's origin and visit a terrible revenge on Iran.

Saudi Arabia, meanwhile, has the money to acquire nuclear weapons and technology on the black market, but possible suppliers are few and very closely watched. To develop the domestic scientific, engineering and industrial base necessary to build a self-sustaining nuclear program would take Saudi Arabia years. In the interim, the Saudis would need nuclear security guarantees from the United States or Europe, which would in turn apply intense pressure on Riyadh not to develop its own arms.

Finally, Turkey may have the resources to build a nuclear weapon, but as a member of the North Atlantic Treaty Organization [NATO], it relied on American nuclear guarantees against the mighty Soviet Union throughout the cold war. There's no obvious reason to presume that American guarantees would seem insufficient relative to Iran.

Examining the Potential Threats

So it seems that while Iranian nuclear weapons might cause considerable disquiet among Iran's neighbors, the United States and other interested parties have many cards to play to limit regional proliferation. But what about the notion that such weapons will facilitate Iranian aggression?

Iranian nuclear weapons could be put to three dangerous purposes: Iran could give them to terrorists; it could use them to blackmail other states; or it could engage in other kinds of aggressive behavior on the assumption that no one, not even the United States, would accept the risk of trying to invade a nuclear state or to destroy it from the air. The first two threats are improbable and the third is manageable.

Would Iran give nuclear weapons to terrorists? We know that Tehran has given other kinds of weapons to terrorists and aligned itself with terrorist organizations, like Hezbollah in Lebanon. But to threaten, much less carry out, a nuclear attack on a nuclear power is to become a nuclear target.

If the Iranians so much as appeared to be readying their nuclear forces for use, the United States might consider a pre-emptive nuclear strike.

Anyone who attacks the United States with nuclear weapons will be attacked with many, many more nuclear weapons. Israel almost certainly has the same policy. If a terrorist group used one of Iran's nuclear weapons, Iran would have to worry that the victim would discover the weapon's origin and visit a terrible revenge on Iran. No country is likely to turn the means to its own annihilation over to an uncontrolled entity.

Because many of Iran's neighbors lack nuclear weapons, it's possible that Iran could use a nuclear capacity to blackmail such states into meeting demands—for example, to raise oil prices, cut oil production or withhold cooperation with the United States. But many of Iran's neighbors are allies of the United States, which holds a strategic stake in their autonomy and is unlikely to sit by idly as Iran blackmails, say, Kuwait or Saudi Arabia. It is unlikely that these states would capitulate to a nuclear Iran rather than rely on an American deterrent threat. To give in to Iran once would leave them open to repeated extortion.

Some worry that Iran would be unconvinced by an American deterrent, choosing instead to gamble that the United States would not make good on its commitments to weak Middle Eastern states—but the consequences of losing a gamble against a vastly superior nuclear power like the United States are grave, and they do not require much imagination to grasp.

Constraining Iran

The final concern is that a nuclear Iran would simply feel less constrained from other kinds of adventurism, including subversion or outright conventional aggression. But the Gulf states can counter Iranian subversion, regardless of Iran's nuclear status, with domestic reforms and by improving their police and intelligence operations—measures these states are, or should be, undertaking in any case.

As for aggression, the fear is that Iran could rely on a diffuse threat of nuclear escalation to deter others from attacking it, even in response to Iranian belligerence. But while it's possible that Iranian leaders would think this way, it's equally possible that they would be more cautious. Tehran could not rule out the possibility that others with more and better nuclear weapons would strike Iran first, should it provoke a crisis or war. Judging from cold war history, if the Iranians so much as appeared to be readying their nuclear forces for use, the United States might consider a pre-emptive nuclear strike. Israel might adopt a similar doctrine in the face of an Iranian nuclear arsenal.

These are not developments to be wished for, but they are risks that a nuclear Iran must take into account. Nor are such calculations all that should counsel caution. Iran's military is large, but its conventional weapons are obsolete. Today the Iranian military could impose considerable costs on an American invasion or occupation force within Iran, but only with vast and extraordinarily expensive improvements could it defeat the American military if it were sent to defend the Gulf states from Iranian aggression.

Each time a new nuclear weapons state emerges, we rightly suspect that the world has grown more dangerous. The weapons are enormously destructive; humans are fallible, organizations can be incompetent and technology often fails us. But as we contemplate the actions, including war, that the United States and its allies might take to forestall a nuclear Iran, we need to coolly assess whether and how such a specter might be deterred and contained.

3

The United States Should Attack Iran to Prevent Its Use of Nuclear Weapons

Norman Podhoretz

Norman Podhoretz is editor-at-large of Commentary, *a monthly magazine of opinion that identifies itself as the flagship of neoconservatism, a political movement that can be distinguished from traditional conservatism by a preference for a proactive approach to protecting national interests. Podhoretz is author of* World War IV: The Long Struggle Against Islamofascism.

Because the goal of Iran's President Mahmoud Ahmadinejad is to destroy Israel and reduce America's global influence, a nuclear Iran poses a serious threat. Deterrence will not prevent Iran's continued pursuit of nuclear weapons as Iran is a nation of religious fanatics who are willing to sacrifice their own people to serve their ideology. Years of diplomacy and sanctions also have failed to stop Iran from pursuing nuclear weapons. The only strategy that is likely to deter Iran from using nuclear weapons is the use of military force. While bombing Iran has its risks, such force is necessary to maintain global security.

The following excerpt was delivered in somewhat different form as an address at a conference, "Is It 1938 Again?" held by the Center for Jewish Studies at Queens College, City University of New York, in April 2007.

Norman Podhoretz, "The Case for Bombing Iran," *Wall Street Journal*, May 30, 2007. Reprinted with permission of the *Wall Street Journal*.

Although many persist in denying it, I continue to believe that what Sept. 11, 2001, did was to plunge us headlong into nothing less than another world war. I call this new war World War IV, because I also believe that what is generally known as the Cold War was actually World War III, and that this one bears a closer resemblance to that great conflict than it does to World War II. Like the Cold War, as the military historian Eliot Cohen was the first to recognize, the one we are now in has ideological roots, pitting us against Islamofascism, yet another mutation of the totalitarian disease we defeated first in the shape of Nazism and fascism and then in the shape of communism; it is global in scope; it is being fought with a variety of weapons, not all of them military; and it is likely to go on for decades.

What follows from this way of looking at the . . . years [following September 11, 2001] is that the military campaigns in Afghanistan and Iraq cannot be understood if they are regarded as self-contained wars in their own right. Instead we have to see them as fronts or theaters that have been opened up in the early stages of a protracted global struggle. The same thing is true of Iran. As the currently main center of the Islamofascist ideology against which we have been fighting since 9/11, and as (according to the State Department's latest annual report on the subject) the main sponsor of the terrorism that is Islamofascism's weapon of choice, Iran too is a front in World War IV. Moreover, its effort to build a nuclear arsenal makes it the potentially most dangerous one of all.

Ahmadinejad's Ambitions

The Iranians, of course, never cease denying that they intend to build a nuclear arsenal, and yet in the same breath they openly tell us what they intend to do with it. Their first priority, as repeatedly and unequivocally announced by their president, Mahmoud Ahmadinejad, is to "wipe Israel off the map"—a feat that could not be accomplished by conventional weapons alone.

But Ahmadinejad's ambitions are not confined to the destruction of Israel. He also wishes to dominate the greater Middle East, and thereby to control the oilfields of the region and the flow of oil out of it through the Persian Gulf. If he acquired a nuclear capability, he would not even have to use it in order to put all this within his reach. Intimidation and blackmail by themselves would do the trick.

Nor are Ahmadinejad's ambitions merely regional in scope. He has a larger dream of extending the power and influence of Islam throughout Europe, and this too he hopes to accomplish by playing on the fear that resistance to Iran would lead to a nuclear war. And then, finally, comes the largest dream of all: what Ahmadinejad does not shrink from describing as "a world without America." Demented though he may be, I doubt that Ahmadinejad is so crazy as to imagine that he could wipe America off the map even if he had nuclear weapons. But what he probably does envisage is a diminution of the American will to oppose him: that is, if not a world without America, he will settle, at least in the short run, for a world without much American influence.

Not surprisingly, the old American foreign-policy establishment and many others say that these dreams are nothing more than the fantasies of a madman. They also dismiss those who think otherwise as neoconservative alarmists trying to drag this country into another senseless war that is in the interest not of the United States but only of Israel. But the irony is that Ahmadinejad's dreams are more realistic than the dismissal of those dreams as merely insane delusions. . . .

Why Deterrence Will Not Work

Listen to what Bernard Lewis, the greatest authority of our time on the Islamic world, has to say . . . on the subject of deterrence:

MAD, mutual assured destruction, [was effective] right through the cold war. Both sides had nuclear weapons. Neither side used them, because both sides knew the other would retaliate in kind. This will not work with a religious fanatic [like Ahmadinejad]. For him, mutual assured destruction is not a deterrent, it is an inducement. We know already that [Iran's leaders] do not give a damn about killing their own people in great numbers. We have seen it again and again. In the final scenario, and this applies all the more strongly if they kill large numbers of their own people, they are doing them a favor. They are giving them a quick free pass to heaven and all its delights.

Nor are they inhibited by a love of country:

We do not worship Iran, we worship Allah. For patriotism is another name for paganism. I say let this land [Iran] burn. I say let this land go up in smoke, provided Islam emerges triumphant in the rest of the world.

These were the words of the Ayatollah Khomeini, who ruled Iran from 1979 to 1989, and there is no reason to suppose that his disciple Ahmadinejad feels any differently.

Still less would deterrence work where Israel was concerned. For as the Ayatollah Rafsanjani (who is supposedly a "pragmatic conservative") has declared:

If a day comes when the world of Islam is duly equipped with the arms Israel has in possession . . . application of an atomic bomb would not leave anything in Israel, but the same thing would just produce damages in the Muslim world.

In other words, Israel would be destroyed in a nuclear exchange, but Iran would survive.

In spite of all this, we keep hearing that all would be well if only we agreed—in the currently fashionable lingo—to "engage" with Iran, and that even if the worst came to the worst we could—to revert to the same lingo—"live" with a nuclear Iran. . . .

The Problem with Diplomacy

But if military force is ruled out, what is supposed to do the job?

Well, to begin with, there is that good old standby, diplomacy. And so, [since 2003], even predating the accession of Ahmadinejad to the presidency, the diplomatic gavotte has been danced with Iran, in negotiations whose carrot-and-stick details no one can remember—not even, I suspect, the parties involved. But since, to say it again, Ahmadinejad is a revolutionary with unlimited aims and not a statesman with whom we can "do business," all this negotiating has had the same result as Munich had with Hitler. That is, it has bought the Iranians more time in which they have moved closer and closer to developing nuclear weapons.

The plain and brutal truth is that if Iran is to be prevented from developing a nuclear arsenal, there is no alternative to the actual use of military force.

The Failed Hope of Sanctions

Then there are sanctions. As it happens, sanctions have very rarely worked in the past. Worse yet, they have usually ended up hurting the hapless people of the targeted country while leaving the leadership unscathed. Nevertheless, much hope has been invested in them as a way of bringing Ahmadinejad to heel. Yet thanks to the resistance of Russia and China, both of which have reasons of their own to go easy on Iran, it has proved enormously difficult for the Security Council to impose sanctions that could even conceivably be effective. At first, the only measures to which Russia and China would agree were much too limited even to bite. Then, as Iran continued to defy Security Council resolutions and to block inspections by the International Atomic Energy Agency [IAEA] that it was bound by treaty to permit, not even the Russians and the Chinese were able to hold out against stronger sanctions. Once more, however, these have had little or no effect on the progress Iran is making toward the development of a nuclear arsenal. On the contrary: they, too, have bought the Iranians additional time in which to move ahead.

Since hope springs eternal, some now believe that the answer lies in more punishing sanctions. This time, however, their purpose would be not to force Iran into compliance, but to provoke an internal uprising against Ahmadinejad and the regime as a whole. Those who advocate this course tell us that the "mullocracy" is very unpopular, especially with young people, who make up a majority of Iran's population. They tell us that these young people would like nothing better than to get rid of the oppressive and repressive and corrupt regime under which they now live and to replace it with a democratic system. And they tell us, finally, that if Iran were so transformed, we would have nothing to fear from it even if it were to acquire nuclear weapons.

A bombing campaign would without question set back [Iran's] nuclear program for years to come.

Once upon a time, under the influence of Bernard Lewis and others I respect, I too subscribed to this school of thought. But after three years and more of waiting for the insurrection they assured us back then was on the verge of erupting, I have lost confidence in their prediction. Some of them blame the [George W.] Bush administration for not doing enough to encourage an uprising, which is why they have now transferred their hopes to sanctions that would inflict so much damage on the Iranian economy that the entire populace would rise up against the rulers. Yet whether or not this might happen under such circumstances, there is simply no chance of getting Russia and China, or the Europeans for that matter, to agree to the kind of sanctions that are the necessary precondition.

The Use of Force

At the outset I stipulated that the weapons with which we are fighting World War IV are not all military—that they also include economic, diplomatic, and other nonmilitary instruments of power. In exerting pressure for reform on countries like Egypt and Saudi Arabia, these nonmilitary instruments are the right ones to use. But it should be clear by now to any observer not in denial that Iran is not such a country. As we know from Iran's defiance of the Security Council and the IAEA even while the United States has been warning Ahmadinejad that "all options" remain on the table, ultimatums and threats of force can no more stop him than negotiations and sanctions have managed to do. Like them, all they accomplish is to buy him more time.

In short, the plain and brutal truth is that if Iran is to be prevented from developing a nuclear arsenal, there is no alternative to the actual use of military force—any more than there was an alternative to force if Hitler was to be stopped in 1938.

The only thing worse than bombing Iran . . . is allowing Iran to get the bomb.

Since a ground invasion of Iran must be ruled out for many different reasons, the job would have to be done, if it is to be done at all, by a campaign of air strikes. Furthermore, because Iran's nuclear facilities are dispersed, and because some of them are underground, many sorties and bunker-busting munitions would be required. And because such a campaign is beyond the capabilities of Israel, and the will, let alone the courage, of any of our other allies, it could be carried out only by the United States. Even then, we would probably be unable to get at all the underground facilities, which means that, if Iran were still intent on going nuclear, it would not have to start over again from scratch. But a bombing campaign would without question set back its nuclear program for years to come, and might even lead to the overthrow of the mullahs.

Answering the Opponents

The opponents of bombing—not just the usual suspects but many both here and in Israel who have no illusions about the nature and intentions and potential capabilities of the Iranian regime—disagree that it might end in the overthrow of the mullocracy. On the contrary, they are certain that all Iranians, even the democratic dissidents, would be impelled to rally around the flag. And this is only one of the worst-case scenarios they envisage. To wit: Iran would retaliate by increasing the trouble it is already making for us in Iraq. It would attack Israel with missiles armed with nonnuclear warheads but possibly containing biological or chemical weapons. There would be a vast increase in the price of oil, with catastrophic consequences for every economy in the world, very much including our own. The worldwide outcry against the inevitable civilian casualties would make the anti-Americanism of today look like a lovefest.

The only prudent—indeed, the only responsible—course is to assume that Ahmadinejad may not be bluffing ... and to strike at him as soon as it is logistically possible.

I readily admit that it would be foolish to discount any or all of these scenarios. Each of them is, alas, only too plausible. Nevertheless, there is a good response to them, and it is the one given by [2008 U.S. Presidential candidate] John McCain.

The only thing worse than bombing Iran, McCain has declared, is allowing Iran to get the bomb.

And yet those of us who agree with McCain are left with the question of whether there is still time. If we believe the Iranians, the answer is no. In early April [2007], at Iran's Nuclear Day festivities, Ahmadinejad announced that the point of no return in the nuclearization process had been reached. If this is true, it means that Iran is only a small step away from producing nuclear weapons. But even supposing that Ahmadinejad is bluffing, in order to convince the world that it is already too late to stop him, how long will it take before he actually turns out to have a winning hand?

If we believe the CIA, perhaps as much as 10 years. But CIA estimates have so often been wrong that they are hardly more credible than the boasts of Ahmadinejad. Other estimates by other experts fall within the range of a few months to six years. Which is to say that no one really knows. And because no one really knows, the only prudent—indeed, the only *responsible*—course is to assume that Ahmadinejad may not be bluffing, or may only be exaggerating a bit, and to strike at him as soon as it is logistically possible.

4

Strong Sanctions Will Prevent Iran from Pursuing Nuclear Weapons

Ivo H. Daalder and Philip H. Gordon

Ivo H. Daalder, a former director for European Affairs on the National Security Council, is a foreign policy fellow at the Brookings Institution and expert on national security affairs, nonproliferation, and nuclear weapons. Philip H. Gordon, also a Brookings fellow and a former director for European Affairs at the National Security Council, is an expert on U.S. strategies for confronting global terrorism and author of Winning the Right War: The Path to Security for America and the World.

The best way to stall Iran's pursuit of nuclear weapons is to impose strong sanctions. Policy makers who believe that Iran is simply pursuing nuclear energy, not weapons, fail to acknowledge the nation's long record of lying about its nuclear program. Those who believe that military force is necessary risk generating popular support in Iran for an already unpopular regime. What the Iranian people want and need are expertise, technology, and integration into the global marketplace, which world leaders should withhold until Iran effectively proves that it has abandoned its nuclear weapons program.

Iran's decision to resume nuclear enrichment activities—a key step in the process of making nuclear weapons—is a direct challenge to the United States, Europe and the rest of the

Ivo H. Daalder and Philip H. Gordon, "We Should Strike Iran, but Not With Bombs," *Washington Post*, January 22, 2006, p. B03. Reproduced by permission of the authors.

world. For more than two years now, Europe—with Washington's support—has offered Tehran a reasonable deal: End the nuclear enrichment work it had been doing in secret for nearly two decades and receive technical support for a civilian nuclear energy program as well as expanded economic and diplomatic ties.

[In January 2006], the new Iranian government of President Mahmoud Ahmadinejad basically told the international community to get lost. It resumed research and development activities that had been suspended during the talks with the Europeans, still claiming that its nuclear program was entirely peaceful. As German Chancellor Angela Merkel made clear on her visit to Washington [in January 2006], even those most committed to a diplomatic solution with Iran now accept that diplomacy has run its course, and the time for decision and action has arrived.

But what decision, and what action? In the debate about how to respond to Iran, two opposing camps have emerged: One wants to give in to Iran; the other wants to bomb it. Both are wrong.

The Danger of Giving In

In the first camp are those—mostly in Europe, but also in many other parts of the world—who accept Tehran's argument that it has a right to develop nuclear technology for peaceful purposes. And while they would oppose an Iranian bomb, they argue that there is little we can do to prevent a determined Iran from building one eventually and that, in any case, a nuclear-armed Iran can be contained. It would be difficult to get international support for economic sanctions, they say, and even if Russia and China were somehow to agree to them, sanctions would fail to change policy—as in Iraq, North Korea and Cuba.

This view is entirely too complacent. It's a delusion to believe that Iran's program is for civilian purposes only and that allowing Iran to master nuclear enrichment is therefore no big deal. Given Iran's long track record of hiding and lying about important aspects of its nuclear program, allowing it to develop enrichment and reprocessing capabilities—even under an international inspection regime—would remove the most important technical barrier to its acquiring nuclear weapons and leave the decision of going nuclear entirely in the hands of Ahmadinejad's radical Islamist government. That is an unacceptable risk.

The United States and Europe . . . should do what they said they would do—make Iran pay a real price if it refuses to suspend its uranium enrichment activities again.

The dangers of an Iranian bomb are clear. Others—Saudi Arabia, Egypt, Turkey—could follow suit, both in order to deter Tehran and in the well-warranted belief that a world that allowed Iran to build a bomb would surely allow them to do so as well. This would be a fatal blow to the already shaky nuclear nonproliferation regime, which for nearly 40 years has helped convince countries as diverse as Sweden, South Korea, Brazil and Ukraine that the costs of acquiring nuclear weapons far outweigh the benefits. Moreover, a nuclear-armed Iran would represent a major threat to regional and global security. It could deter the United States and others from responding to Iranian aggression or to Tehran's support for terrorism in the Middle East and beyond. And given the messianic streak of Tehran's current leaders, do we really want to run the risk of them passing nuclear materials or even a weapon on to al Qaeda?

The Risks of Military Force

On the other side of the debate are those—mostly in the United States—who think that the time has come to use military force against Iran. Because diplomacy has failed and we are, as President [George W.] Bush has said, "all sanctioned-out" as far as Iran is concerned, the only option left is a military strike against Iran's nuclear facilities before it is too late. If ever there were a case, they argue, for making good Bush's vow—that America will "not allow the world's most dangerous regimes to possess . . . the world's most dangerous weapons"—this is it.

This view, too, is wrong. U.S. air strikes probably could destroy Iran's critical nuclear facilities—at least those we know about. But our intelligence is hardly perfect, so we would not really know if Tehran's nuclear program was in fact destroyed. A military attack against Iran would also undoubtedly generate strong public support among Iranians for an otherwise unpopular regime. Any lingering doubt that they needed a nuclear deterrent would be erased.

And are we prepared for what Iran could do in return? Through its Shiite partners in Iraq and Afghanistan, it could wreak havoc on our forces and undermine our efforts to stabilize both countries. It could threaten oil shipments through the Strait of Hormuz, through which more than one-third of the world's oil flows, and urge its terrorist friends to launch retaliatory strikes against our allies and us.

If Americans and Europeans are unwilling to run the risk of a temporary rise in oil prices as part of what it takes to prevent an Iranian bomb, then they had better be prepared to live with the consequences.

The option of relying on Israel to strike Iranian targets—as alluded to [in 2005] by Vice President Cheney—would be even worse. The Israelis would conduct the operation less effectively because of their more limited military means (striking targets in eastern Iran would be a stretch for Israel's limited-range F-15s), and the United States would bear the responsibility anyway, not least if it allowed the Israelis to fly over U.S.-controlled airspace in Iraq.

Making Iran Pay a Real Price

Given these bad options, what should the United States and Europe do instead? The answer is that they should do what they said they would do—make Iran pay a real price if it refuses to suspend its uranium enrichment activities again. This means first making a concerted effort to win Russian and Chinese support for tough action at the International Atomic Energy Agency and the U.N. Security Council. Ideally, the Security Council should not only denounce Iran's actions but agree on an oil embargo and a ban on investment in Iran.

The credibility of sanctions would be enhanced if it were clear that negotiations could resume—and punitive actions be suspended—as soon as Tehran terminates the enrichment activities it recently resumed. The offer to support a civilian nuclear energy program, increase trade and investment—and even engage in regional security talks and restore diplomatic relations with the United States—would also remain on the table.

Serious sanctions would slow the nuclear program by squeezing the Iranian economy and cutting off key technologies.

But if Tehran refuses to back down, it must pay a price. And while Russia and China may not go along, Europe, Japan and the United States should not hide behind their refusal. The argument that sanctions won't work without China, Russia and India on board is overstated. Only Western companies at present possess the sort of expertise and technology that Iran's energy sector needs, and in an integrated world oil market, whatever oil China and India purchase from Iran liberates supplies elsewhere. Iran could, of course, retaliate by pulling its oil off the world market, which would cause a price spike. But if Americans and Europeans are unwilling to run the risk of a temporary rise in oil prices as part of what it takes to prevent an Iranian bomb, then they had better be prepared to live with the consequences as well.

The Iranian government believes, as Ahmadinejad put it recently, that "you [the West] need us more than we need you." Do we really want to encourage him in this belief?

There is no guarantee that making the threat of sanctions more credible or actually imposing them will have an immediate and positive effect, but given the alternatives it certainly makes sense to find out. And even if sanctions don't work in the short term, they would still be useful to give future Iranian leaders an incentive to cooperate and to send a message to other potential proliferators. At the very least, serious sanctions would slow the nuclear program by squeezing the Iranian economy and cutting off key technologies, would further strain the already disgruntled middle classes who might one day push the current regime aside, and would serve as leverage in the future if Iran ever does decide to engage the West.

Iran must be presented with a clear choice: It can become an impoverished, isolated pariah state with nuclear weapons—like North Korea—or it can begin to reintegrate with the international community, meet the needs of its people and preserve its security in exchange for forgoing this capability. The choice will be for the Iranians to make. But we must force them to make it.

5

Israel May Preemptively Strike Iran to Prevent Its Use of Nuclear Weapons

Peter Brooks

Peter Brooks, a senior fellow at the Heritage Foundation, a conservative think tank, is a former deputy assistant secretary of defense who also served in the Navy and with the Central Intelligence Agency.

While Iran maintains that it is producing uranium to supply the nation's energy needs, Israeli intelligence has drawn a different conclusion. Israel believes that Iran is producing highly enriched uranium for nuclear weapons. Some experts assert that based on this belief, Israel may preemptively strike Iran's nuclear facilities. Israel has in fact attacked nuclear facilities in Iraq and Syria. Despite the significant challenges of such a strike, Israel could be successful. Israeli leaders have on many occasions clearly stated that Israel would never allow its enemies to use weapons of mass destruction against its people.

In late December [2007], Tehran [Iran] crowed that its 1,000-megawatt Bushehr nuclear plant, supposedly meant to produce peaceful nuclear energy, would be "online" as early as this spring, cementing in place another important building block of its questionable nuclear program.

While the builders of the Bushehr plant, the Russians, insist the plant will not be completed until the end of [2008],

Peter Brooks, "Israel vs. Iran: 1st Strike Strategies," *The Heritage Foundation*, February 12, 2008. Reproduced by permission.

Moscow did make the first of several deliveries of fuel rods to Iran in late December [2007].

This unwelcome news comes as Iran is continuing to spin as many as 3,000 centrifuges to enrich uranium, ostensibly to produce low-enriched uranium reactor fuel, but which could also be used to make highly enriched uranium (HEU) for nuclear weapons.

Indeed, while Iran is planning for some 50,000 centrifuges, some experts believe that just these 3,000, if running efficiently and 24/7, could produce enough HEU for one bomb in a year.

Enter Israel

This sort of news cannot help but rattle even the steadiest of policymakers' nerves, no matter what the narrowly focused National Intelligence Estimate (NIE) said about the current dormant state of Iran's nuclear weapons program—especially in a country like Israel. While Israeli intelligence reportedly has no new—or different—information than that contained in the American intelligence assessment, it draws a very different conclusion than the U.S.: Israel believes the weapons program continues. You have to wonder, then, if Israel—the country most threatened by an Iranian nuclear (weapons) breakout—might take matters into its own hands. It has done so at least once, and maybe twice, before. And considering that an American strike on Iran's nuclear facilities is likely off the table for the moment, due to the NIE, the time may be here—again—for the Israelis to take action.

Indeed, Lt. Gen. Gabi Ashkenazi, the Israeli Defense Forces' (IDF) chief of staff, said at a December [2007] conference in Tel Aviv: "It's up to the international community to act in a determined way to stop Iran's nuclearization. . . . But at the same time we have the responsibility to prepare for any scenario in the event that international efforts do not succeed."

That sort of no-nonsense, self-help attitude seems to be backed up by the IDF's record against regional nuclear programs that the Israelis have perceived as serious threats to their national security. In a 1981 dawn raid lasting less than 90 seconds, IDF fighters attacked the nearly completed 40-megawatt Iraqi Osirak nuclear reactor complex south of Baghdad, setting back Saddam Hussein's ability to produce fissile material for nuclear weapons. And again in September [2007], the IDF appears to have struck a nascent Syrian nuclear program, which was possibly benefiting from outside help, in a preventive airstrike that may have also been meant as a warning to Iran of unpleasantries to come.

Eyes on Iran

So, could Iran be next? It just might be, especially considering the new timelines revealed by the Iranians involving the construction, fueling and initial operating capability of Bushehr—not to mention an influx of new weaponry. It is possible that within about a year of Bushehr becoming operational, some of its spent nuclear fuel could be stripped of enough plutonium to produce a handful of nuclear weapons if the rods are not returned, as agreed, to their owner/supplier, Russia.

While these challenges to an [Israeli Defense Forces] preventive strike against Iranian nuclear targets are significant, the mission . . . could be a success.

Because the production of sufficient fissile material is the most challenging task in constructing a nuclear weapon, the diversion of material at Bushehr is potentially as big a problem as the 3,000 centrifuges Iran has currently whirring at supersonic speeds, enriching uranium.

Attacking Bushehr—like Osirak—before it comes online would not only stop it from being used to produce fissile material for weapons, but would also prevent radiation from being spewed into the atmosphere after a strike.

Also possibly spurring the Israeli government into action sooner rather than later is other recent unpleasant news: Iran's defense minister announced in December [2007] that Tehran is buying the highly capable Russian S-300 air-defense system. The sale of the strategic S-300 (SA-10/Grumble) will complement the $700 million in Tor-M1 (SA-15/Gauntlet) short-range surface-to-air missile systems Moscow supplied [in 2007], further enhancing Iran's air defense network. (The Russian defense ministry denied the sale of military equipment to Iran in a likely effort to avoid unnecessarily further cooling Moscow's already frosty relations with Washington—or roiling the water with other regional countries concerned with such a transfer.)

Iran likely purchased the Tor-M1 to stave off a repeat of Israel's success against Osirak—or the possibility that the U.S., well-suited for an air- or sea-based strike, would take action against Iran's nuclear program. The long-range S-300s—likely a response to the IDF's September [2007] strike on Syrian facilities—will enhance Iran's ability to protect its nuclear sites scattered around the country, some of which are already ringed with air defenses. (While understandable, considering the saber-rattling coming from a number of corners, it is curious the extent to which Iran is willing to go to protect its so-called "peaceful" nuclear program with military might.)

Iran is also suspected of possibly having a new ballistic missile, the Ashura, with a 1,200-mile range, capable of reaching Israel—and beyond. It is not clear whether the missile is being produced, or has, in fact, been tested by Iran, as Tehran claimed in late November [2007].

Tyrannies of Targeting

But despite these possible proximate reasons for the Israeli government giving the "go-ahead" for an attack on Bushehr before it is up and running, successfully dealing militarily with Iran's nuclear program is no small task. First, while Bushehr is certainly a key element in Iran's vast nuclear program, due to its ability to produce large amounts of bomb-worthy fissile material (i.e., plutonium) for weapons use, it is not the only element that needs to be addressed. To cripple—or at least set back—Iran's nuclear program, the IDF would have to hit other major sites: the Natanz uranium enrichment plant, the Arak heavy water facility and the Isfahan uranium conversion complex, plus, possibly, tens of other nuclear-related sites around the country. (The Iranians are also reportedly building a 40-megawatt research reactor at Arak, which, like Osirak, is too small for power production, but just right for the production of plutonium from its spent fuel, according to experts.)

There's also the tyranny of distance. Iran is a lot farther from Israel than Iraq—and the targets are not conveniently clustered like at Osirak. They're spread across Iran—a country nearly four times the size of California (or neighboring Iraq). Since key targets are out of range of Israel's ballistic missiles, the routing of strike packages would also present significant challenges. This raid would be more difficult that the Osirak raid in which IDF fighters slipped with impunity along the Jordanian and Saudi borders. Besides the most likely flight skirting Jordan and Saudi Arabia en route to Iran, IDF fighters could also go through or along the borders of Turkey (a friendly country) or Syria (a nonfriendly country), or a combination thereof, pushing flight routes of about 1,200 miles.

The Challenge of Secrecy

Secrecy would be a problem, too. While Israel has good operational security—witness how much is still unknown about the Syrian raid—an airstrike would require an armada of fighter, tanker, airborne early warning and electronic intelligence aircraft, which would light up radars across the region.

Even an uncoordinated, surprise Israeli air raid would likely quickly be known to others, especially the U.S., which "owns" the airspace in the Middle East and the Persian Gulf with its vast array of land, sea and air platforms and sensors. (Considering the geography, the possibility of unintended engagements between U.S. and Israeli forces almost eliminates the possibility of no notice being given to U.S. command authorities before a strike is launched.)

Many of the potential targets in the Iranian nuclear set, like the Natanz uranium enrichment facility, are also hardened, located near population centers and even buried as far down as 70 feet below ground. Plus, the Iranians are not likely to take this lying down. In addition to ground-based air defenses, including SA-5s and I-Hawk, the Iranian Air Force will throw an assortment of aging air assets at the Israelis, including MiG-29s, Su-24/25s, F-14s, F-4s, F-5s, F-7s and F-1s.

Moreover, an Israeli strike would severely complicate regional politics, especially for the U.S., which is (incorrectly) seen as Israel's handler. An attack by the Jewish state on a Muslim country, even troublesome Iran, would not be taken well at all in the region, especially on the "street." The situation would be further exacerbated, especially in some quarters of Iraq, if it were perceived—or it were actually the case—that the U.S. allowed the IDF to use parts of Iraqi airspace for, or turned a blind eye to, an attack on neighboring Iran.

Mission Impossible?

While these challenges to an IDF preventive strike against Iranian nuclear targets are significant, the mission, if embarked upon by Israel as a matter of national security, could be a success. The Israelis could advise the Americans of the strike in advance, allowing the two sides to deconflict their forces and providing a degree of freedom of movement in the gulf area for the IDF to operate if Washington supported the effort. Regional Arab states likely would not intervene, even if they became aware of the raid in progress. But they would protest vociferously after the strike, while privately breathing a sigh of relief, considering concerns surrounding an ascendant Iran.

The green light for an attack is militarily doable if Israel perceives Tehran's Iranian nuclear weapons program might lead to [the] notion that Israel must be 'wiped off the map.'

Depending on the level of tactical engagement with the Iranians, the Israeli fighters, especially the F-15s, have the range to hit key targets. Precision-guided and penetration weapons such as JDAMs would likely be effective against hardened and buried targets. Nukes—as some have suggested— would not be necessary. But, the distances involved could limit the loiter time of Israeli fighters for dealing with emerging targets, especially those that might be involved in a counterstrike against Israel, such as Shahab-class road-mobile ballistic missiles. Of course, Israel's small fleet of cruise missile-capable, Dolphin-class diesel submarines, deployed to the Persian Gulf, could play an important role in a strike, especially against Bushehr in southern Iran. Israeli commandos could also play a role.

Persian Payback

Another issue that has to be taken into account by Israeli policymakers is that an IDF strike on Iran almost certainly would bring Iranian retaliation in a number of forms against Israel and its interests in the region—and beyond. Israel could expect Iranian ballistic-missile attacks against large cities such as Haifa and Tel Aviv as well as conventional and terrorist attacks by Tehran's allies, Hezbollah or Hamas. And Syria could get into the act. (By association, U.S. interests could come into Iran's crosshairs, too.)

The next chapter of Iran's nuclear weapons program is not yet written, but Israeli policymakers and defense planners do not need to be reminded that a single nuclear weapon is enough to destroy the small Jewish state—and its 7 million people. What is clear is that an Israeli strike on Iranian nuclear facilities would not be easy or ideal—not to mention pregnant with plenty of potential negative consequences, for Israel, the U.S. and peace and stability in the Middle East more broadly. Indeed, while a strike might push back the Iranian nuclear program, it will not necessarily deter Tehran from continuing to pursue its atomic dreams: The Osirak raid served to steel Saddam's resolve to get the bomb, according to his former bomb makers.

But the green light for an attack is militarily doable if Israel perceives Tehran's Iranian nuclear weapons program might lead to Iranian President Mahmoud Ahmadinejad's notion that Israel must be "wiped off the map." The words of Israel's Menachem Begin government after the Osirak raid must still ring in the ears of Israel's policymakers today: "Under no circumstances will we allow an enemy to develop weapons of mass destruction against our people."

[2008] will likely bring more unhappy news about Iran's nuclear program as it cascades toward a weapons option. It will also be a fateful year for Israel, one that may require action against Iran—no matter what the NIE says.

6

Israel Should Not Preemptively Strike Iran

Bernard Avishai and Reza Aslan

Bernard Avishai, who covered the Middle East as a journalist, has written extensively on the Middle East and is the author of The Hebrew Republic: How Secular Democracy and Global Enterprise Will Bring Israel Peace at Last. *Reza Aslan, a writer and scholar of religions, is a fellow at the University of Southern California's Center on Public Diplomacy and is Middle East analyst for CBS News. He is also the author of* No god but God: The Origins, Evolution, and Future of Islam.

If Israel does indeed intend to attack Iran's nuclear sites, it should reexamine the reasoning behind such a plan. Iranian President Mahmoud Ahmadinejad's ambitions to attack Israel are simply political rhetoric to distract the Iranian people from its domestic problems. Ahmadinejad has no power over Iran's nuclear program. The real power in Iran lies with the mullahs who recognize that to develop, Iran must open its doors to the global marketplace. Moreover, Iran's nuclear program is not as fully developed as some believe. Threats of an Israelis attack on Iran only increase Iranian solidarity and keep the nation closed to the world.

Bernard Avishai and Reza Aslan, "An Israeli Strike on Iran, a Plan That Just Doesn't Fly," *Washington Post*, August 10, 2008, p. B03. Reproduced by permission of the authors.

The Bush administration seems less and less likely to launch a parting strike on Iran's nuclear installations—but Israel isn't sounding nearly so tranquil. The talk from Jerusalem will almost certainly grow more strident as the competition to replace the country's scandal-plagued prime minister, Ehud Olmert[1], intensifies. Former Israeli defense minister Shaul Mofaz is running hard against the less hawkish Foreign Minister Tzipi Livni to succeed Olmert as leader of the governing Kadima Party; he recently told Israel's dominant daily newspaper, *Yediot Ahronot*, that an attack on Iran was "unavoidable." And Binyamin Netanyahu, the right-wing opposition leader who might well beat either Livni or Mofaz in a general election, is also likely to think seriously about a preventive Israeli raid.

Iran presents the West with a kind of real-life chess game, and the advocates of a preemptive Israeli attack only understand checkers.

An Existential Threat?

Meanwhile, prominent Israeli military analysts, officials and writers are insisting that Iran constitutes a mounting "existential threat." Take one of the country's most important historians, the erstwhile dove Benny Morris, who recently predicted in the *New York Times* that "Israel will almost surely attack Iran's nuclear sites in the next four to seven months"— roughly (and not inconveniently) the period between the U.S. presidential election and the departure of the Bush administration. Morris claimed that his view that Israel's existence was on the line is shared "across the political spectrum." In Israel

---

1. Olmert resigned in July 2008 after months of mounting pressure over corruption allegations. Olmert is the subject of two criminal investigations: (1) suspicion that he took bribes from the American businessman, Morris Talansky, and (2) that he submitted duplicate claims for travel expenses in his previous posts as trade minister and mayor of Jerusalem.

today, anyone who resists such talk risks becoming an appeaser amid a chorus of Churchills.[2]

Leave aside the possibility that the threat of an Israeli attack may be designed to give leverage to U.S. and European diplomats pressuring Iran to abandon its nuclear efforts. Leave aside the question of whether, if you believed that such a strike was truly imminent, you'd predict it in a major newspaper. Leave aside the fact that no Israeli strike could happen without a U.S. green light and permission to fly over Iraq. And leave aside the perennial suspicions that Israel's military elite, which sees the Jewish state as the West's foremost strategic asset in the region, also tends to see the Middle East through the prism of the "dash of civilizations" between Islam and the West. Could Israeli threats be serious?

Challenging the Underlying Premises

We hope not, because we don't buy the underlying premises. Here's the argument one hears almost daily in Israel: Iranian President Mahmoud Ahmadinejad is a jihadist fanatic; he is bent on (as he put it) wiping Israel "off the map," and his insistence on denying the Holocaust shows that he may be vile enough to perpetrate another one; the Iranian regime is on the fast track to developing a nuclear weapon. So the West—and if not the West, then Israel alone—must treat Iran as though it were the national equivalent of a suicide bomber. It must strike now, without hesitation, before it's too late.

The idea that one fine morning Iran will incinerate Tel Aviv is madness.

Moreover, the argument continues, even if a nuclear-armed Iran didn't attack Israel first, it would still spur an arms race

2. Following World War I and during the rise of Hitler and Nazi Germany, many politicians were in favor of appeasement. Winston Churchill, however, believed that Germany menaced freedom and democracy and that appeasement amounted "to the complete surrender of the Western Democracies to the Nazi threat of force."

that would turn the region into a nest of mutually assured destroyers that would include Egypt and Saudi Arabia. An Iranian bomb would also curtail Israel's freedom of action if it has to strike against the tens of thousands of missiles now in the hands of Hezbollah, Iran's fearsome proxy in southern Lebanon. So why should Israel not . . . just go for broke?

Here's why not: because Iran presents the West with a kind of real-life chess game, *and* the advocates of a preemptive Israeli attack only understand checkers. Intelligence experts insist that we examine both the intentions and the capabilities of an opponent. Let's do that.

Examining Intentions

The president of Iran is not the regime. Ahmadinejad has almost no control over Iran's nuclear program; that power rests in the hands of the country's supreme leader, Ayatollah Ali Khamenei. Khamenei alone commands Iran's military and dictates its foreign policy. Through intermediaries such as Vice President Esfandiar Rahim-Mashaei, Khamenei has adopted a much softer tone than Ahmadinejad on nuclear negotiations with the West. As Rahim-Mashaei recently put it, according to Iranian news agencies, "Iran wants no war with any country, and today Iran is a friend of the United States and even Israel."

Israeli threats to attack Iran produce only paranoia and solidarity inside Iran.

The Iranian regime is not a suicide bomber. The idea that one fine morning Iran will incinerate Tel Aviv is madness; Morris's description of the mullahs' "fundamentalist, self-sacrificial mindset," echoed by others, is a caricature. The Iranian regime knows full well that Israel has an arsenal widely thought to include as many as 200 nuclear warheads as well as missiles, submarines, strategic bombers and enough apocalyptic psyches to retaliate. Do Israelis seriously believe that Iranians hate them (on behalf of the Palestinians, who would be poisoned by the fallout) more than they love their children—or, for that matter, the historic cities of Tehran, Qom and Esfahan?

The regime wants to survive. The mullahs, let us remember, have managed to remain in power for three decades, despite international isolation, a devastating eight-year war with Iraq and the loathing of the vast majority of the country's citizens. In times of economic frustration, they rely on anti-Israeli and anti-American gambits to distract attention from domestic hardship; we should view their nuclear program in this context. This is a country that sits atop the world's third-largest proven reserves of oil, according to the CIA, yet imports about 40 percent of its gasoline—simply because it doesn't have the resources or the know-how to update its refineries to pump more. We have greater reason to assume that, in time, the mullahs will bow to internal pressure and open their country to global intellectual capital than to think that they will engage in an ecstasy of suicidal mass murder.

The Iranian nuclear program is daring but not crazy. Consider the view from Tehran. The United States overthrew Iran's government in 1953 to obtain Iranian oil, and the country is now surrounded by U.S. troops—in Iraq, Afghanistan, Kuwait, Qatar and the United Arab Emirates. This surely argues for prudence from Tehran. Besides, the regime has probably learned a valuable lesson from another member of the "axis of evil": Nuclear North Korea was never attacked; it was offered hundreds of millions of dollars to give up its bombs. Nuclear diplomacy, the mullahs have probably concluded, enhances the international prestige of what would otherwise be a Third World country.

Examining Capabilities

An Iranian bomb need not precipitate a regional nuclear arms race. Israel's bomb—developed by the Middle Eastern power most hated and feared by its neighbors—hasn't.

Even if Tehran were determined to get the bomb, there's no guarantee that it could pull it off. Iran's nuclear program is far more modest than its leaders like to admit. As undersecretary of State William Burns testified before Congress [in July 2008], "It is apparent that Iran has not yet perfected [uranium] enrichment, and as a direct result of U.N. sanctions, Iran's ability to procure technology or items of significance to its missile programs . . . is being impaired."

An Iranian bomb will not "degrade Israel's deterrence." Tens of thousands of conventional missiles in southern Lebanon, Syria, Gaza—and Iran—have already done that. Hezbollah knows that it can bombard Israel and survive, as it did during its summer 2006 war with Israel. If an Iranian bomb would provide cover for Hezbollah, Hamas and their state sponsors to launch these missiles at some indefinite point in the future, but a preemptive Israeli attack on Iran would make Iran's proxies launch them now (as Hezbollah did two years ago), how exactly does the logic of regaining Israeli "deterrence" work?

None of these points mean that Ahmadinejad will stop blustering; he is a two-bit politician playing to his base. Nor does it mean that the Western powers should stop planning a long-term strategy of containing Iran. But Western powers should now focus not only on their power to deter but on their power to attract; we should push for new collective-security agreements that would benefit everyone in the region. Israeli threats to attack Iran produce only paranoia and solidarity inside Iran. And after 40 years of Israeli occupation in Palestine, Israel's threats also have the handy effect of changing the subject.

7

North Korea Is Taking Steps to End Its Nuclear Weapons Program

George W. Bush

George W. Bush, the forty-third president of the United States, included North Korea in an "axis of evil" in his January 29, 2002, State of the Union address. Relations have been tense between the Bush administration and the North Korean regime. After North Korea withdrew from the Nuclear Non-Proliferation Treaty in 2003, meetings known as the "six-party talks" began with six participating states—the People's Republic of China, the Republic of Korea (South Korea), the Democratic People's Republic of Korea (North Korea), the United States of America, the Russian Federation, and Japan. These meetings led to the pledges Bush discusses in the following viewpoint.

Although the United States will continue to keep a watchful eye on North Korea's nuclear intentions, North Korea took a major step by agreeing to disable its nuclear facilities and openly declare its nuclear activities. In return, the United States will lift some of the sanctions against North Korea and will remove North Korea from its list of state sponsors of terrorism. Sanctions for North Korea's human rights violations and its 2006 nuclear test, however, will remain in place. If North Korea fails to live up to its promises, the nation will have to accept the consequences.

George W. Bush, "Press Release: President Bush Discusses North Korea," whitehouse.gov, June 26, 2008.

The policy of the United States is a Korean Peninsula free of all nuclear weapons. [On June 26, 2008] we moved a step closer to that goal, when North Korean officials submitted a declaration of their nuclear programs to the Chinese government as part of the six-party talks.

The United States has no illusions about the regime in Pyongyang. We remain deeply concerned about North Korea's human rights abuses, uranium enrichment activities, nuclear testing and proliferation, ballistic missile programs, and the threat it continues to pose to South Korea and its neighbors.

North Korea ... pledged to declare its nuclear activity [and] ... has begun describing its plutonium-related activities.

A First Step

Yet we welcome today's development as one step in the multistep process laid out by the six-party talks between North Korea, China, Japan, Russia, South Korea, and the United States.

North Korea pledged to disable its nuclear facilities. North Korea has begun disabling its Yongbyon nuclear facility—which was being used to produce plutonium for nuclear weapons. This work is being overseen by officials from the United States and the IAEA [International Atomic Energy Agency]. And to demonstrate its commitment, North Korea has said it will destroy the cooling tower of the Yongbyon reactor in front of international television cameras [June 27, 2008].

[In 2007] North Korea also pledged to declare its nuclear activity. With today's declaration, North Korea has begun describing its plutonium-related activities. It's also provided other documents related to its nuclear programs going back to 1986. It has promised access to the reactor core and waste facilities at Yongbyon, as well as personnel related to its nuclear program. All this information will be essential to verifying that North Korea is ending its nuclear programs and activities.

Action for Action

The six-party talks are based on a principle of "action for action." So in keeping with the existing six-party agreements, the United States is responding to North Korea's actions with two actions of our own:

First, I'm issuing a proclamation that lifts the provisions of the Trading with the Enemy Act with respect to North Korea.

And secondly, I am notifying Congress of my intent to rescind North Korea's designation as a state sponsor of terror in 45 days. The next 45 days will be an important period for North Korea to show its seriousness of its cooperation. We will work through the six-party talks to develop a comprehensive and rigorous verification protocol. And during this period, the United States will carefully observe North Korea's actions—and act accordingly.

The two actions America is taking will have little impact on North Korea's financial and diplomatic isolation. North Korea will remain one of the most heavily sanctioned nations in the world. The sanctions that North Korea faces for its human rights violations, its nuclear test in 2006, and its weapons proliferation will all stay in effect. And all United Nations Security Council sanctions will stay in effect as well.

The six-party process has shed light on a number of issues of serious concern to the United States and the international community. To end its isolation, North Korea must address these concerns. It must dismantle all of its nuclear facilities, give up its separated plutonium, resolve outstanding questions on its highly enriched uranium and proliferation activities, and end these activities in a way that we can fully verify.

North Korea must also meet other obligations it has undertaken in the six-party talks. The United States will never forget the abduction of Japanese citizens by the North Koreans. We will continue to closely cooperate and coordinate with Japan and press North Korea to swiftly resolve the abduction issue.

A Moment of Opportunity

This can be a moment of opportunity for North Korea. If North Korea continues to make the right choices, it can repair its relationship with the international community—much as Libya has done over the past few years. If North Korea makes the wrong choices, the United States and our partners in the six-party talks will respond accordingly. If they do not fully disclose and end their plutonium, their enrichment, and their proliferation efforts and activities, there will be further consequences.

Multilateral diplomacy is the best way to peacefully solve the nuclear issue with North Korea. Today's developments show that tough multilateral diplomacy can yield promising results. Yet the diplomatic process is not an end in itself. Our ultimate goal remains clear: a stable and peaceful Korean Peninsula, where people are free from oppression, free from hunger and disease, and free from nuclear weapons. The journey toward that goal remains long, but today we have taken an important step in the right direction.

8

North Korea's Efforts to End Its Nuclear Weapons Program Are Inadequate

Jayshree Bajoria

Jayshree Bajoria is a staff writer for the Council on Foreign Relations, a think tank that offers diverse opinions on issues concerning foreign relations.

While many believe that North Korea's efforts to account for its nuclear weapons program are an important first step, others claim that the North Korean regime has no intention of giving up its pursuit of nuclear weapons. Critics contend that North Korea's declaration fails to provide adequate details of its uranium enrichment program. Moreover, these experts argue, the account of its nuclear program does not adequately address the nation's proliferation of nuclear technology. Indeed, some assert that North Korea's goal is simply to obtain political and economic benefits. According to these critics, appeasement only increases the likelihood of future confrontation.

In a significant move in North Korea's denuclearization process, Pyongyang turned in a long-overdue account of its nuclear program to Chinese officials. The Bush administration immediately responded by lifting the provisions of the Trading with the Enemy Act and notifying Congress of its intention to remove North Korea from the State Sponsors of Terrorism list in the next forty-five days. Yet critics of the

Jayshree Bajoria, "Pyongyang's Deal," *Council on Foreign Relations—Daily Analysis*, June 27, 2008. Copyright © 2008 by the Council on Foreign Relations, Inc. All rights reserved. Reproduced by permission.

declaration say the report, which only details plutonium-based materials and facilities, falls short on three important counts:

- It does not include details of suspected uranium enrichment;

- It does not address Pyongyang's proliferation activities to countries like Syria and Libya;

- It fails to give an account of the nuclear weapons already produced.

Experts have long argued that the North Korean regime ... does not have any intention of giving up its nuclear program completely.

Capitulating to Pyongyang

The exchange ... amounts to far less than the Bush administration's goals when it originally agreed to this formula during the Six-Party Talks. But after a compromise in April [2008], the United States appears to have softened its stance on the issue amid criticisms of capitulating to Pyongyang. That has brought mixed reactions domestically, though some Democrats who have been highly critical of the pace of Bush diplomacy toward North Korea took solace in what they saw as a snub of the hard-liners who drove policy for much of Bush's tenure.

U.S. Secretary of State Condoleezza Rice, in a *Wall Street Journal* op-ed, argues the policy will get Kim Jong-Il's regime out of the plutonium-making business, which she calls "by far its largest nuclear effort." Rice acknowledges the real challenge ahead is verification of the accuracy and completeness of declaration, and says the sanctions will be reimposed if North Korea is found to have cheated. President Bush also sought to silence hard-liners, saying lifting sanctions off North Korea "will have little impact on North Korea's financial and diplomatic isolation."

A Symbolic Gesture

The Bush administration has suggested it will try to verify the contents of the declaration during the forty-five-day period it takes for North Korea to be officially removed from the list of state sponsors of terrorism, but experts say the verification will likely take months to complete. In a move meant to underscore the decision to decommission part of its nuclear program, Pyongyang imploded the cooling tower of the Yongbyon nuclear plant [June 27, 2008], offering the world an unusual opportunity to witness live a step in the diplomatic process. This is a largely symbolic gesture, writes Jon Wolfsthal, senior fellow at the Washington-based Center for Strategic and International Studies. "None of the steps North Korea has taken thus far are irreversible, but the destruction of this tower makes it harder to reconstitute their plutonium program," he writes.

As a U.S.-designated state sponsor of terrorism, North Korea faces a range of economic and trade restrictions. The removal of sanctions will make it eligible for financial assistance from the international financial institutions. "Whether they get that support is a different matter," says CFR's [Council on Foreign Relation's] Gary Samore. Also, he says, it does not change much in bilateral trade relations. "American business is not clamoring to invest in North Korea even if the sanctions are lifted," he says.

Experts have long argued that the North Korean regime intends to use the denuclearization process to gain political and economic benefits, but does not have any intention of giving up its nuclear program completely. Winston Lord of the International Rescue Committee and former CFR president Leslie H. Gelb wrote in an April [2008] *Washington Post* editorial that yielding to North Korea will only increase the likelihood of confrontation down the line. But, they say, "feeling the glow of a rare foreign policy accomplishment," President [George W.] Bush "may proceed to cement a legacy."

Still, Samore argues this is a useful initial step. "We can't ignore North Korea, we can't force it to give up its nukes, so the only strategy that is left is the incremental quid pro quo strategy," he says.

9

The United States Can Contain Nuclear Proliferation in Pakistan

Michael Krepon

Michael Krepon, cofounder of the Henry L. Stimson Center, a foreign policy and national security think tank, worked for the U.S. Arms Control and Disarmament Agency during the Jimmy Carter administration. He also worked at the Carnegie Endowment for International Peace and is author of the Better Safe than Sorry: The Ironies of Living with the Bomb.

The fear that Islamic extremists will take over the Pakistani government and use the nation's nuclear weapons against its enemies is unwarranted. The United States has several strategies it can use to help Pakistan safely manage its nuclear arsenal. The United States can recommend ways to improve nuclear security, but must do so at a safe distance so that the Pakistanis do not think the United States plans to seize Pakistan's nuclear assets. The best strategy is to help improve economic conditions in Pakistan, which will in turn increase the nation's stability.

[P]akistan's] weapons are the nation's most closely guarded man-made objects, its "crown jewels," so to speak. I do not place much credence in scenarios that project a takeover of the Pakistani government or Army leadership by Islamic extremists. Pakistan's religious parties do not fare well in national elections. The most hard-core Islamic extremists have

Michael Krepon, "How Safe and Secure are Pakistan's Nuclear Weapons?" Stimson.org, June 12, 2008. Reproduced by permission.

turned against their former handlers in Pakistan's military and security services, but they are in no position to take over the state. Acts of Muslim-on-Muslim violence, especially those that claim the lives of innocent bystanders, do not win hearts and minds.

Evaluating the Threats

If the takeover threat by extremists is overblown, what developments in Pakistan would most threaten the safety and security of Pakistan's "crown jewels"? One possibility is a breakdown of the unity of command within the Pakistan Army. Another is a serious crisis or a military clash with neighboring India.

The United States can . . . help promote nuclear safety and security on the Subcontinent by acting as a crisis manager if and when Pakistan and India again go eyeball to eyeball.

When tensions rise precipitously with India, the readiness level of Pakistan's nuclear deterrent also rises. The dictates of deterrence mandate some movement of launchers and weapons from fixed locations during crises. Nuclear weapons on the move are inherently less secure than nuclear weapons at heavily guarded storage sites and are also more susceptible to "insider" security threats. If a crisis spills over into combat, the possibility of a mushroom cloud, whether by accident, a breakdown of command and control, or a deliberate, top-down decision cannot be discounted.

How likely is this scenario? A horrific act of violence that sparks another serious crisis on the Subcontinent is always a possibility. However, the Pakistan Army leadership can be expected to try to avoid having heightened security concerns on two fronts. This means that, as long as activities along the border with Afghanistan preoccupy Pakistan's military and intelligence services, they will seek to avoid serious tensions with India.

The Pakistan Army's unity of command is essential for nuclear security. Thus, a second worrisome scenario is a prolonged period of turbulence and infighting among the country's President, Prime Minister, and Army Chief. Under the current Pakistani Constitution, the President picks the Army Chief. But Pakistan's Constitution is far from being a settled document, and one of the amendments currently under consideration would shift this important prerogative to the Prime Minister. The President is also the head of Pakistan's National Command Authority, as presently constituted. This, too, might change in the event of a shift of power in favor of the Prime Minister.

The triangular jockeying for power in Pakistan isn't new. At times, political leaders have chosen Army Chiefs, but their track record has not been good. Unwelcome outcomes usually result when Pakistani Army Chiefs are elevated to help advance political agendas rather than by their seniority and professionalism.

Pakistan's Army reflects popular sentiment. It follows that, if national governments do not address popular grievances, those grievances will grow, including within the Army. If national divisions widen, they will also widen within the military.

The Role of the United States

What, then, can the United States do to help Pakistan improve its nuclear safety and security? There is very great suspicion in Pakistan about U.S. intentions. Mistrust grows with every press report or idle comment about U.S. contingency plans to "seize" or otherwise take action against Pakistan's nuclear assets in the event of an imminent breakdown of governmental authority or a prospective rise of Islamist extremists into leadership positions. Such speculation reinforces the natural instinct of Pakistani military authorities to keep U.S. officials at a safe distance from their crown jewels. This, in turn, limits the amount and kind of security assistance that the Pakistani authorities are willing to accept.

The most effective measures to promote nuclear safety and security are those that help Pakistan to find its footing.

Providing "best practices" on how to improve security at sensitive sites is possible from a safe distance: The United States doesn't need to visit such facilities in order to impart the lessons we have learned based on long experience. Nor does it require classified sensors and technologies to upgrade the security perimeters at sensitive sites. Pakistani authorities are more likely to accept U.S. offers of assistance that meet the "safe distance" rule and are pursued in a low-profile way.

The United States can also help promote nuclear safety and security on the Subcontinent by acting as a crisis manager if and when Pakistan and India again go eyeball to eyeball. Crisis avoidance and peace making are far, far better than crisis management. Regrettably, Washington has focused very little on ways to promote a Kashmir settlement and reconciliation between India and Pakistan.

Over the long haul, the most effective measures to promote nuclear safety and security are those that help Pakistan to find its footing. A well governed, stable society that is at peace with its neighbors is one in which nuclear weapons have little use and are well guarded. The United States can help Pakistan's military to counter threats to internal security, but this will take time—and a reorientation of a Pakistani military mindset that has previously focused on India rather than on internal security.

The United States can't build a more stable, well governed Pakistan—this is the job of Pakistanis. But U.S. policies toward South Asia can still influence outcomes, even if they don't determine them.

Retrieving U.S. standing in Pakistan will be a long, hard slog, since American interests are now widely viewed as pro-Musharraf and anti-Pakistan. Political stability and good governance will be slow in coming. These goals will not be advanced by U.S. disengagement. Congress can help Pakistan to find its footing by providing bottom-up, non-military assistance programs that manifestly improve standards of living within the country. Military assistance programs that help Pakistan's armed forces to counter the common threat of Islamic extremism would also be wise investments in the future.

10

The Threat of Nuclear Terrorism Is Real

Matthew Bunn

Matthew Bunn is associate professor of public policy and coprincipal investigator in the Project on Managing the Atom at Harvard University's John F. Kennedy School of Government. During the Bill Clinton administration, Bunn served as an adviser to the Office of Science and Technology Policy, where he played a major role in U.S. policies related to the control and disposition of weapons-usable nuclear materials in the United States and the former Soviet Union. Bunn is the author of Securing the Bomb 2007.

Intelligence reveals that terrorists want access to nuclear weapons, and appalling worldwide nuclear security measures make it plausible that terrorists could gain access to the materials needed to build them. The theft of highly enriched uranium, the material used in nuclear bombs, is not fiction, but reality. If terrorists were to use stolen materials to set off a bomb, millions would be killed and the economic and political fallout would be devastating. While no terrorists are currently known to have a nuclear weapon, efforts to improve security of nuclear materials will go a long way to prevent the disastrous risks of their ever obtaining them.

Matthew Bunn, "The Risk Of Nuclear Terrorism—And Next Steps To Reduce The Danger," *Testimony for the Committee on Homeland Security and Governmental Affairs, United States Senate*, April 2, 2008. Reproduced by permission of the author.

Several basic questions can give us an understanding of the risk of nuclear terrorism.

The Bad News

Do terrorists want nuclear weapons? For a small set of terrorists, the answer is clearly "yes." Osama bin Laden has called the acquisition of nuclear weapons or other weapons of mass destruction a "religious duty." Al Qaeda operatives have made repeated attempts to buy nuclear material for a nuclear bomb, or to recruit nuclear expertise—including the two extremist Pakistani nuclear weapon scientists who met with bin Laden and Ayman al-Zawahiri to discuss nuclear weapons. Before al Qaeda, the Japanese terror cult Aum Shinrikyo also made a concerted effort to get nuclear weapons. With at least two groups going down this path in the last 15 years, we must expect that others will in the future.

Is it plausible that a sophisticated terrorist group could make a crude nuclear bomb if they got HEU [highly enriched uranium] or separated plutonium? The answer here is also "yes." Making at least a crude nuclear bomb might well be within the capabilities of a sophisticated group, though a nuclear bomb effort would be the most technically challenging operation any terrorist group has ever accomplished. One study by the now-defunct congressional Office of Technology Assessment summarized the threat: "A small group of people, none of whom have ever had access to the classified literature, could possibly design and build a crude nuclear explosive device . . . Only modest machine-shop facilities that could be contracted for without arousing suspicion would be required." Indeed, even before the revelations from Afghanistan, U.S. intelligence concluded that "fabrication of at least a 'crude' nuclear device was within al-Qa'ida's capabilities, if it could obtain fissile material."

A terrorist cell of relatively modest size, with no large fixed facilities that would draw attention, might well be able to pull off such an effort—and the world might never know until it was too late.

Could a terrorist group plausibly get the material needed for a nuclear bomb? Unfortunately, the answer here is also "yes." Nuclear weapons or their essential ingredients exist in hundreds of buildings in dozens of countries, with security measures that range from excellent to appalling—in some cases, no more than a night watchman and a chain-link fence. No specific and binding global standards for how these stockpiles should be secured exist.

Theft of [highly enriched uranium] and plutonium is not a hypothetical worry, it is an ongoing reality.

A Lack of Nuclear Security

Remarkably, another thing that does not exist is a comprehensive, prioritized list of which nuclear stockpiles around the world pose the highest risks of nuclear theft—though the Nuclear Material Information Program (NMIP), led by one of your earlier witnesses, Rolf Mowatt-Larsen, is working to create one. Based on the information we do have in the public domain, I believe the highest risks of nuclear theft today are in the former Soviet Union, in Pakistan, and at HEU-fueled research reactors around the world. . . .

HEU-fueled research reactors typically have comparatively modest stockpiles of material—but they have some of the world's weakest security measures for those stocks. And it is important to remember that much of the irradiated fuel from research reactors is still HEU, and is not radioactive enough to pose any significant deterrent to theft by suicidal terrorists. Some 130 research reactors around the world still use HEU as their fuel.

While these are the highest-risk categories, virtually every country where these materials exist—including the United States—has more to do to ensure that these stocks are effectively protected against the kinds of threats that terrorists and criminals have shown they can pose.

Theft of HEU and plutonium is not a hypothetical worry, it is an ongoing reality. Most recently, in February 2006, Russian citizen Oleg Khinsagov was arrested in Georgia (along with three Georgian accomplices) with some 100 grams of 89% enriched HEU, claiming that he had kilograms more available for sale. What we do not know, of course, is how many thefts may have occurred that were never detected; it is a sobering fact that nearly all of the stolen HEU and plutonium that has been seized over the years had never been missed before it was seized.

The amounts required for a bomb are small. The Nagasaki bomb included some 6 kilograms of plutonium, which would fit easily in a soda can. A similar HEU bomb would require three times as much. For a simpler but less-efficient gun-type design, roughly 50 kilograms of HEU would be needed— roughly the size of a six-pack. The world stockpiles of HEU and separated plutonium are enough to make roughly 200,000 nuclear weapons; a tiny fraction of one percent of these stockpiles going missing could cause a global catastrophe.

The Threat to the United States

Could a terrorist group likely deliver a bomb to Washington, New York, or other major cities around the world? Here, too, unfortunately, the answer is "yes." If stolen or built abroad, a nuclear bomb might be delivered to the United States, intact or in ready-to-assemble pieces, by boat or aircraft or truck. The length of the border, the diversity of means of transport, the vast scale of legitimate traffic across national borders, and the ease of shielding the radiation from plutonium or especially from HEU all operate in favor of the terrorists. Building the overall system of legal infrastructure, intelligence, law enforcement, border and customs forces, and radiation detectors needed to find and recover stolen nuclear weapons or materials, or to interdict these as they cross national borders, is an extraordinarily difficult challenge.

It is a sobering thought that a nuclear effort might not require a conspiracy larger than the one which perpetrated the 9/11 attacks and succeeded in remaining secret.

What would happen if terrorists set off a nuclear bomb in a U.S. city? Here, the answers are nothing short of terrifying. A bomb with the explosive power of 10,000 tons of TNT (that is, 10 "kilotons," somewhat smaller than the bomb that obliterated Hiroshima), if set off in midtown Manhattan on a typical workday, could kill half a million people and cause roughly $1 trillion in direct economic damage. Terrorists— either those who committed the attack or others—certainly would claim they had more bombs already hidden in U.S. cities (whether they did nor not), and the fear that this might be true could lead to panicked evacuations of major U.S. cities, creating widespread havoc and economic disruption. If the bomb went off in Washington, D.C., large fractions of the federal government would be destroyed, and effective governance of the country would be very much in doubt. Devastating economic aftershocks would reverberate throughout the country and the world—global effects that in 2005 then-UN Secretary-General Kofi Annan warned would push "tens of millions of people into dire poverty," creating "a second death toll throughout the developing world." America and the world would be transformed forever—and not for the better.

The Good News

Fortunately, there is good news in this story as well. First, there is no convincing evidence that any terrorist group has yet gotten a nuclear weapon or the materials needed to make one—or that al Qaeda has yet put together the expertise that would be needed to make a bomb. Indeed, there is some evidence of confusion and lack of nuclear knowledge by some senior al Qaeda operatives.

Second, making and delivering even a crude nuclear bomb would be the most technically challenging and complex operation any terrorist group has ever carried out. There would be many chances for the effort to fail, and the obstacles may seem daunting even to determined terrorists, leading them to focus more of their efforts on conventional tools of terror—as al Qaeda appears to have done. Both al Qaeda and Aum Shinrikyo appear to have encountered a variety of difficulties, demonstrating that getting a nuclear bomb is a difficult challenge, even for large and well-financed terrorist groups with ample technical resources.

Third, the overthrow of the Taliban and the disruption of al Qaeda's old central command structure certainly reduced al Qaeda's chances of pulling off such a complex operation—though that capability may be growing again, as al Qaeda reconstitutes in the mountains of Pakistan.

Fourth, nuclear security is improving. While there is a great deal yet to be done, the fact is that at scores of sites in Russia, the former Soviet Union, and elsewhere, security is dramatically better than it was fifteen years ago. Security upgrades are scheduled to be completed for most Russian nuclear warhead and nuclear material sites by the end of [2008]. HEU is being removed from sites all around the world, permanently eliminating the risk of nuclear theft at those sites. An alphabet soup of programs and initiatives—Cooperative Threat Reduction (CTR), the Materials Protection, Control, and Accounting (MPC&A) program, the Global Threat Reduction Initiative (GTRI), the Global Initiative to Combat Nuclear Terrorism (GI), the International Atomic Energy Agency's Office of Nuclear Security, the Domestic Nuclear Detection Office

(DNDO), and many more—are each making real contributions. There can be no doubt that America and the world face a far lower risk of nuclear terrorism today than they would have had these efforts never been begun. These programs are excellent investments in U.S. and world security, deserving strong support; Americans and the world owe a substantial debt of gratitude to the dedicated U.S., Russian, and international experts who have been carrying them out. Securing the world's stockpiles of nuclear weapons and the materials needed to make them is a big job, and a complex job, but it is a doable one, as the progress already made demonstrates.

The danger of nuclear terrorism is high enough to have a significant effect on the life expectancy of everyone who lives and works in downtown Washington or midtown Manhattan.

Fifth, hostile states are highly unlikely to consciously choose to provide nuclear weapons or the materials needed to make them to terrorist groups. Such a decision would mean transferring the most awesome military power the state had ever acquired to a group over which it had little control, and potentially opening the regime to overwhelming retaliation—a particularly unlikely step for dictators or oligarchs obsessed with controlling their states and maintaining power.

All of this good news comes with a crucial caveat: "as far as we know." The gaps in our knowledge remain wide. Some intelligence analysts argue that the lack of hard evidence of an extensive current al Qaeda nuclear effort simply reflects al Qaeda's success in compartmentalizing the work and keeping it secret. It is a sobering thought that a nuclear effort might not require a conspiracy larger than the one which perpetrated the 9/11 attacks and succeeded in remaining secret—and that Aum Shinrikyo was simply not on the radar of any of the world's intelligence agencies until *after* they perpetrated their nerve gas attack in the Tokyo subways.

What Is the Probability of Nuclear Terrorism?

So, taking the good news with the bad, what are the chances of a terrorist nuclear attack? The short answer is that nobody knows. Former Secretary of Defense William Perry and former Assistant Secretary of Defense Graham Allison are among those who have estimated that chance at more than 50% over the next ten years. In 2006, I published a mathematical model that provides a structured, step-by-step way of thinking through the problem. A set of plausible illustrative values for the input parameters resulted in a 29% 10-year probability estimate—by coincidence, the same as the median estimate of the 10-year probability of a nuclear attack on the United States in a survey of national security experts by Senator Lugar's office some years ago. Since there are large uncertainties in each of those inputs, however, the real probability could well be either higher or lower. But if these estimates are even within a factor of 3–5 of being correct, and if, as I believe, there is a large chance that such an attack would be directed at Manhattan or Washington, D.C., then the danger of nuclear terrorism is high enough to have a significant effect on the life expectancy of everyone who lives and works in downtown Washington or midtown Manhattan.

Even a 1% chance over the next ten years would be enough to justify substantial action to reduce the risk, given the scale of the consequences. No one in their right mind would operate a nuclear power plant upwind of a major city that had a 1% chance over ten years of blowing sky-high—the risk would be understood by all to be too great. But that, in effect, is what we are doing—or worse—by managing the world's nuclear stockpiles as we do today.

11

Fears That Terrorists Will Obtain Nuclear Weapons Are Misplaced

Sonia Ben Ouagrham-Gormley

Sonia Ben Ouagrham-Gormley, a senior project manager with the Center for Nonproliferation Studies, is editor-in-chief of the NIS Export Control Observer, a monthly newsletter devoted to analysis of weapons of mass destruction export control issues in newly independent states (NIS). Ben Ouagrham-Gormley is also an adjunct professor at the School of Advanced International Studies, Johns Hopkins University, where she teaches a course on weapons of mass destruction in the former Soviet Union.

A focus on the security of nuclear materials and access to the knowledge required to create nuclear weapons diverts policy makers from the actual threat posed by terrorists and the states that sponsor them. Acquiring the designs and instructions needed to create nuclear weapons is relatively easy. The greatest challenge is obtaining the specialized knowledge needed to create them. Moreover, while there is in fact a black market for nuclear materials, most smugglers are intercepted and the stolen material in most transactions is not useful to build a nuclear weapon. Indeed, focusing on nuclear vulnerabilities ignores the actual capabilities of terrorists.

Sonia Ben Ouagrham-Gormley, "Nuclear Terrorism's Fatal Assumptions," *Bulletin of the Atomic Scientists*, October 22, 2007. Reproduced by permission of Bulletin of the Atomic Scientists. www.thebulletin.org.

In a casual, often-irreverent tone, journalist William Langewiesche walked readers of the December 2006 issue of *The Atlantic* through the possibilities and hurdles associated with procuring the required material for a nuclear weapon, transporting it to a safe place, and assembling the bomb. With no ambitions to provide solutions to these questions, his article was a pretext to draw attention to the successes and failures of U.S. assistance to Russia and other former Soviet states in protecting fissile material, safeguarding borders, identifying trafficking routes, and exposing the involvement of local criminal groups.

Langewiesche diverges from the conventional wisdom: The odds of terrorist success are very slim, he concludes. Yet he, like many other journalists and researchers, makes two assumptions that neglect important qualifying factors that would improve our understanding of a state's or terrorist group's capability to acquire nuclear weapons or dirty bombs.

It took Manhattan Project scientists with explicit knowledge of physics and possession of fissile material considerable time to design and construct a workable and reliable . . . nuclear weapon.

The Challenge of Obtaining Nuclear Knowledge

The first and most common assumption is that procuring material and equipment is the largest obstacle. Most reports fall prey to the simplistic notion that globalization and the internet have made scientific knowledge virtually universal: Once the material is in hand, states or terrorist groups are merely a few steps away from their goal.

Specialized know-how, however, is difficult to come by. Knowledge can be divided generally into two categories: explicit knowledge (information or instructions that can be formulated in words, symbols, formulas, or diagrams and can be easily transferred) and tacit knowledge (unarticulated, personally held knowledge or skills that a scientist or technician acquires and transfers through a practical, hands-on process and direct interactions with other scientists).

Explicit information such as designs and instructions cannot be efficiently used in the absence of the related tacit knowledge. Science and technology scholars have demonstrated that it took Manhattan Project scientists with explicit knowledge of physics and possession of fissile material considerable time to design and construct a workable and reliable prototype implosion nuclear weapon. First they needed to solve a multitude of difficult engineering and interdisciplinary scientific problems, which required hiring thousands of technical specialists to develop a unique knowledge base and building an extensive, indigenous infrastructure.

The vast majority of materials involved in documented trafficking transactions have no application in a nuclear weapon or dirty bomb.

The novelty of nuclear technology was not the sole challenge. Soviet scientists encountered significant problems replicating the U.S. design and production process obtained from Soviet spy Klaus Fuchs, even though they already had an active nuclear program with knowledgeable scientists and engineers. The British encountered similar problems, even though their scientists contributed to the Manhattan Project. Each country's program had the character of an independent invention.

More recently, bioweapons research illustrated the critical role that specialized know-how plays in transferring existing technologies to a new environment. It took Soviet scientists at the Stepnogorsk bioweapons production plant about five years to design and produce a weaponizable strain of anthrax in the late 1980s despite about 400 pages of protocols describing the development and production of earlier Soviet anthrax weapons, samples of an anthrax strain developed at the Kirov bioweapons facility, and the transfer of 65 senior bioweaponeers from other weapons sites.

Questioning the Existence of a Nuclear Black Market

The focus on material leads to a second widespread assumption: the existence of a nuclear black market in the former Soviet Union. After the Soviet Union's dissolution, former member states inherited an enormous amount of nuclear and radioactive material, which has been the source of a number of trafficking incidents. Revelations about the nuclear network of Pakistani scientist A.Q. Khan only reinforced trepidations of a burgeoning black market in the region, adding concerns that organized crime might coalesce with this market to channel nuclear material to terrorists.

While [authorities are] focusing on vulnerability-based analyses of the nuclear threat, the true capabilities of terrorists or states are overlooked.

Before concluding anything about the nature of a nuclear black market in the former Soviet Union, it is useful to consider the qualities of markets in general. At the very least, a market consists of a transaction between a supplier and a client and the transportation and financial mechanisms that allow goods and funds to circulate. The Khan network possessed these features. With an established clientele, a network of suppliers, transport and funding mechanisms that evaded scrutiny, and direct contacts between Khan or his suppliers and their clients, the network provided a flexible list of equipment and expert services that clients could choose from.

The supposed nuclear black market in the former Soviet Union lacks an important component of any market: an established clientele. According to the James Martin Center for Nonproliferation Studies's Illicit Trafficking Database and publications, most nuclear transactions are conducted by isolated suppliers—primarily economic opportunists—who have no clients at the outset, and blindly probe the underground world to identify potential buyers. An analysis of 183 cases that occurred between 2001 and 2006 in the former Soviet Union also showed that traffickers transport their goods along various routes—an east-west route from Russia, Ukraine, and Belarus to Europe; a southwest corridor crossing Central Asia and the Caucasus toward Europe; and a southeast corridor, from Central Asia to neighboring Asian and Mideast countries—presuming the existence of a demand in countries along the way. These smugglers are usually intercepted before reaching their declared destination, caught while transporting the goods, crossing a border, or during the sale of the material (often to an undercover agent).

No Clear Connection

Additionally, the vast majority of materials involved in documented trafficking transactions have no application in a nuclear weapon or dirty bomb, and their value is typically overestimated. Fifty percent of trafficking incidents between 2001 and 2006 concerned radioactive orphan sources, contaminated scrap metal, and radioactive isotopes. Accounts of these incidents rarely indicate the exact quantity or quality of the radioactive material, making it difficult to evaluate the significance of the incident; the analysis of these cases showed, however, that most of them involve industrial instruments that typically contain small quantities of radioactive material. Among the 10 reported incidents involving highly enriched uranium (HEU), only 3 involved weapon-grade material enriched to 80 percent or more. And in these cases, the total material amounted to gram-quantities (5 grams, 170 grams, and 100 grams), hardly enough material for a weapon, which requires at least 10 to 15 *kilograms* of HEU.

The data-set shows no clear nexus between trafficking, organized crime, and terrorism. Three incidents have involved undocumented connections with terrorist organizations, and 12 cases have a crime-group connection. These cases, however, display the same amateurish features as the rest of the data-set, and involve small quantities of material—such as Osmium 187, low enriched uranium, and depleted uranium—that have no weapons or dirty bomb application. Only one incident involved both weapon-grade HEU and a crime connection.

With these examples, one can see how focusing on access to materials dangerously mischaracterizes the challenges that terrorists and states face in pursuing nuclear weapons. The general emphasis on explicit scientific knowledge, rather than the highly specialized know-how derived from extensive hands-on experience is similarly misleading. While [authorities are] focusing on vulnerability-based analyses of the nuclear threat, the true capabilities of terrorists or states are overlooked.

12

The United States Should Aggressively Promote Nuclear Disarmament

George P. Shultz, William J. Perry, Henry A. Kissinger, and Sam Nunn

Former U.S. Secretary of State George P. Shultz is professor of international economics at the Graduate School of Business at Stanford University and a fellow at the Hoover Institution. William J. Perry, also a fellow at the Hoover Institution and a Stanford University professor, is codirector of the Preventive Defense Project, a research collaboration of Stanford and Harvard universities. Former U.S. Secretary of State Henry A. Kissinger is chairman of Kissinger Associates, an international consulting firm. Former chairman of the Senate Armed Services Committee, Sam Nunn is currently cochairman and chief executive officer of the Nuclear Threat Initiative (NTI), a charitable organization working to reduce the global threats from nuclear, biological, and chemical weapons.

Cold-war style deterrence will not prevent nuclear proliferation, as evidenced by North Korea's 2006 nuclear test and Iran's refusal to discontinue its uranium enrichment programs. The United States should therefore take the lead in pursuing the goal of a world free of nuclear weapons envisioned by many prominent world leaders. The United States should make achieving this goal a joint enterprise in which all nations agree to take ur-

gent steps such as reducing the size of nuclear forces, halting global production of fissile materials, and improving nuclear security standards. The success of this global effort will determine the security of future generations.

Nuclear weapons today present tremendous dangers but also a historic opportunity. U.S. leadership will be required to take the world to the next stage—to a solid consensus for reversing reliance on nuclear weapons globally as a vital contribution to preventing their proliferation into potentially dangerous hands, and ultimately ending them as a threat to the world.

Nuclear weapons were essential to maintaining international security during the Cold War because they were a means of deterrence. The end of the Cold War made the doctrine of mutual Soviet-American deterrence obsolete. Deterrence continues to be a relevant consideration for many states with regard to threats from other states. But reliance on nuclear weapons for this purpose is becoming increasingly hazardous and decreasingly effective.

A Dangerous New Era

North Korea's recent nuclear test and Iran's refusal to stop its program to enrich uranium—potentially to weapons grade— highlight the fact that the world is now on the precipice of a new and dangerous nuclear era. Most alarming, the likelihood that nonstate terrorists will get their hands on nuclear weaponry is increasing. In today's war waged on world order by terrorists, nuclear weapons are the ultimate means of mass devastation. And nonstate terrorist groups with nuclear weapons are conceptually outside the bounds of a deterrent strategy and present difficult new security challenges.

Apart from the terrorist threat, unless urgent new actions are taken, the United States soon will be compelled to enter a new nuclear era that will be more precarious, psychologically disorienting, and economically costly than Cold War deterrence. It is far from certain that we can successfully replicate the old Soviet-American "mutually assured destruction" with an increasing number of potential nuclear enemies worldwide without dramatically increasing the risk that nuclear weapons will be used. New nuclear states do not have the benefit of years of step-by-step safeguards put in effect during the Cold War to prevent nuclear accidents, misjudgments, or unauthorized launches. The United States and the Soviet Union learned from mistakes that were less than fatal. Both countries were diligent to ensure that no nuclear weapon was used during the Cold War by design or by accident. Will new nuclear nations and the world be as fortunate in the next 50 years as we were during the Cold War?

A Long-Desired Goal

Leaders addressed this issue in earlier times. In his "Atoms for Peace" address to the United Nations in 1953, Dwight D. Eisenhower pledged America's "determination to help solve the fearful atomic dilemma—to devote its entire heart and mind to find the way by which the miraculous inventiveness of man shall not be dedicated to his death, but consecrated to his life." John F. Kennedy, seeking to break the logjam on nuclear disarmament, said, "The world was not meant to be a prison in which man awaits his execution."

Rajiv Gandhi, addressing the U.N. General Assembly on June 9, 1988, appealed: "Nuclear war will not mean the death of a hundred million people. Or even a thousand million. It will mean the extinction of four thousand million: the end of life as we know it on our planet earth. We come to the United Nations to seek your support. We seek your support to put a stop to this madness."

Ronald Reagan called for the abolishment of "all nuclear weapons," which he considered to be "totally irrational, totally inhumane, good for nothing but killing, possibly destructive of life on earth and civilization." Mikhail Gorbachev shared this vision, which had also been expressed by previous American presidents.

Although Reagan and Gorbachev failed at Reykjavik [a summit meeting between the two leaders in Reykjavik, Iceland] to achieve the goal of an agreement to get rid of all nuclear weapons, they did succeed in turning the arms race on its head. They initiated steps leading to significant reductions in deployed long- and intermediate-range nuclear forces, including the elimination of an entire class of threatening missiles.

What will it take to rekindle the vision shared by Reagan and Gorbachev? Can a worldwide consensus be forged that defines a series of practical steps leading to major reductions in the nuclear danger? There is an urgent need to address the challenge posed by these two questions.

First and foremost should be intensive work with leaders of the countries in possession of nuclear weapons to turn the goal of a world without nuclear weapons into a joint enterprise.

Nonproliferation Efforts

The Non-Proliferation Treaty (NPT) envisioned the end of all nuclear weapons. It provides that states that did not possess nuclear weapons as of 1967 agree not to obtain them, and that states that do possess them agree to divest themselves of these weapons over time. Every president of both parties since Richard Nixon has reaffirmed these treaty obligations, but states without nuclear weapons have grown increasingly skeptical of the sincerity of the nuclear powers.

Strong nonproliferation efforts are under way. The Cooperative Threat Reduction Program, the Global Threat Reduction Initiative, the Proliferation Security Initiative, and the Additional Protocols are innovative approaches that provide powerful new tools for detecting activities that violate the NPT and endanger world security. They deserve full implementation. The negotiations on proliferation of nuclear weapons by North Korea and Iran, involving all the permanent members of the Security Council plus Germany and Japan, are crucially important. They must be energetically pursued.

But by themselves, none of these steps are adequate to the danger. Reagan and Gorbachev aspired to accomplish more at their meeting in Reykjavik 20 years ago—the elimination of nuclear weapons altogether. Their vision shocked experts in the doctrine of nuclear deterrence but galvanized the hopes of people around the world. The leaders of the two countries with the largest arsenals of nuclear weapons discussed the abolition of their most powerful weapons.

What should be done? Can the promise of the NPT and the possibilities envisioned at Reykjavik be brought to fruition? We believe that a major effort should be launched by the United States to produce a positive answer through concrete stages. First and foremost should be intensive work with leaders of the countries in possession of nuclear weapons to turn the goal of a world without nuclear weapons into a joint enterprise. Such a joint enterprise, by involving changes in the disposition of the states possessing nuclear weapons, would lend additional weight to efforts already underway to avoid the emergence of a nuclear-armed North Korea and Iran.

Reassertion of the vision of a world free of nuclear weapons ... would be perceived as a bold initiative consistent with America's moral heritage.

Taking Urgent Steps

The program on which agreements should be sought would constitute a series of agreed-on and urgent steps that would lay the groundwork for a world free of the nuclear threat. Such steps would include:

- Changing the Cold War posture of deployed nuclear weapons to increase warning time and thereby reduce the danger of an accidental or unauthorized use of a nuclear weapon.

- Continuing to reduce substantially the size of nuclear forces in all states that possess them.

- Eliminating short-range nuclear weapons designed to be forward-deployed.

- Initiating a bipartisan process with the Senate, including understandings to increase confidence and provide for periodic review, to achieve ratification of the Comprehensive Test Ban Treaty, taking advantage of recent technical advances and working to secure ratification by other key states.

- Providing the highest possible standards of security for all stocks of weapons, weapons-usable plutonium, and highly enriched uranium everywhere in the world.

- Getting control of the uranium enrichment process, combined with the guarantee that uranium for nuclear power reactors could be obtained at a reasonable price, first from the Nuclear Suppliers Group and then from the International Atomic Energy Agency (IAEA) or other controlled international reserves. It will also be necessary to deal with proliferation issues presented by spent fuel from reactors producing electricity.

- Halting the production of fissile material for weapons globally, phasing out the use of highly enriched uranium in civil commerce, and removing weapons-usable uranium from research facilities around the world and rendering the materials safe.

- Redoubling our efforts to resolve regional confrontations and conflicts that give rise to new nuclear powers. Achieving the goal of a world free of nuclear weapons will also require effective measures to impede or counter any nuclear-related conduct that is potentially threatening to the security of any state or peoples.

Reassertion of the vision of a world free of nuclear weapons and practical measures toward achieving that goal would be, and would be perceived as, a bold initiative consistent with America's moral heritage. The effort could have a profoundly positive impact on the security of future generations. Without the bold vision, the actions will not be perceived as fair or urgent. Without the actions, the vision will not be perceived as realistic or possible.

We endorse setting the goal of a world free of nuclear weapons and working energetically on the actions required to achieve that goal, beginning with the measures outlined above.

13

The United States Should Resurrect the Comprehensive Test-Ban Treaty

Michael O'Hanlon

Michael O'Hanlon is a senior fellow at the Brookings Institution, where he has authored or coauthored books on defense policy, including The Future of Arms Control. *O'Hanlon specializes in U.S. national security policy and is senior author of the* Iraq Index. *He spent five years at the Congressional Budget Office specializing in nuclear weapons issues.*

To promote nonproliferation of nuclear weapons, the United States should resume support for the Comprehensive Test-Ban Treaty. Test-ban treaty supporters must assure critics that nuclear tests can be actually detected and therefore verified. Advocates must also explain that a test-ban treaty will not reduce the reliability of the current U.S. nuclear arsenal because a warhead's reliability can be determined without tests. Proponents can remind doubters that efforts to reduce testing have convinced many nations, such as Japan, Argentina, and Germany, not to pursue nuclear weapons. Indeed, a test-ban treaty would go a long way toward preventing new nuclear states.

The [1996 Comprehensive Test-Ban Treaty] has been explicitly identified by many non-nuclear-weapons states as their top priority in recent years. More specifically, it is what they demand out of the established nuclear powers as a condi-

Michael O'Hanlon, "Resurrecting the Test-Ban Treaty," *Survival*, vol. 50, February-March 2008, pp. 120–127, 130–132. Reproduced by permission of Taylor & Francis, Ltd., www.tandf.co.uk/journals and the author.

tion for their continued willingness to forgo nuclear weapons themselves, while also agreeing to place their civilian nuclear programmes under the additional protocol of the International Atomic Energy Agency [IAEA] (that provides for thorough inspections of facilities), and ideally also agreeing to obtain nuclear fuel for civilian reactors from an international fuel bank rather than their own enrichment or reprocessing capabilities. The indefinite extension of the Nuclear Non-Proliferation Treaty was achieved by the world community in 1995, according to the man who presided over the decision-making process, 'largely because the long-stalled comprehensive test ban ... seemed at last certain of adoption'. The test-ban treaty is thus directly linked to stopping nuclear proliferation. Even though it has been out of the headlines for several years, the continuing importance of the treaty is not easily exaggerated. With a US presidential campaign underway, and a new American president to be inaugurated fairly soon, the issue demands renewed attention and vigorous bipartisan debate.

Advocates of the treaty can at least be relieved about one thing: none of what [President George W.] Bush has done in regard to the treaty is irreversible. The president did not 'unsign' the treaty; he also has not tested nuclear weapons during his tenure in office and is unlikely to do so before leaving the White House. His administration has periodically sought funds to research new types of nuclear warheads that would likely require testing somewhere down the road, yet these research efforts have been severely constrained by Congress. Whatever harm has resulted to the nuclear non-proliferation regime over the past seven years, notably the 2003 North Korean nuclear breakout and 2006 test, was probably not due primarily to American policy on nuclear testing. . . . There is thus reason to think that the next American president might resume the push for a comprehensive ban on nuclear weapons testing, a goal of nuclear arms-control and non-proliferation advocates for half a century.

> *Efforts to reduce testing and reduce arsenals over the last four decades have helped convince governments ... not to pursue these weapons.*

Answering the Challenges

There are huge challenges to be addressed before any such agenda can be realised. At the US domestic political level, while it was [George W.] Bush who wished to undo the treaty, it was the Republican Senate of the late 1990s that opposed its ratification. . . . They raised questions that will have to be answered if a future ratification vote is to gain the support of 10–15 Republican members, the minimum that will likely be needed to ensure its passage and to establish a strong bipartisan support for a ban on nuclear testing in the future.

The key questions about the treaty are these: can such a treaty be verified? Does it really help enhance the non-proliferation agenda, and if so, how? Does it allow the United States to ensure the long-term reliability of its existing arsenal in a manner that provides robust deterrence for the country and its allies? Finally, to the extent that might be judged necessary, is the treaty consistent with future American nuclear-weapons needs, such as the possible development of 'bunker buster' nuclear devices designed for deep underground detonation? All of these questions are serious. All have been considered before. But the standard answers given by test-ban advocates have not always been the strongest or most convincing. In addition, in some cases, the situation has changed in light of new geostrategic conditions and technical advances. . . .

Is a Treaty Verifiable?

Large nuclear-weapons detonations are easy to detect. If in the atmosphere (in violation of the 1963 partial test-ban treaty) they are visible by satellite, and their characteristic radiation distribution makes them easy to identify. It is largely for such reasons that no country trying to keep its nuclear capabilities secret has tested in the atmosphere in the modern era. If the detonations are underground, as is more common, they are still straightforward to identify via seismic monitoring, provided they reach a certain size. Any weapon of kilotonne power or above (the Hiroshima and Nagasaki bombs were in the 10–20kt range) can be 'heard' in this way. In other words, any weapon with significant military potential tested at its full strength is very likely to be noticed. American seismic arrays are found throughout much of Eurasia's periphery, for example, and even tests elsewhere could generally be picked up. Indeed, though it either 'fizzled' or was designed to have a small yield in the first place, with a yield of about 1kt and thus well below those of the Hiroshima and Nagasaki bombs, the October 2006 North Korean test was detected and clearly identified as a nuclear burst. . . .

US nuclear verification capabilities have picked up the Indian, Pakistani and North Korean nuclear tests (even the small, relatively unsuccessful ones) in the last decade and would be able to do so with high confidence for tests from those or other countries in the future. Verification capabilities are not airtight or perfect, but their limitations are on balance not grounds to oppose a comprehensive test ban.

Would the Treaty Help the Nonproliferation Agenda?

It cannot really be true, critics of the Comprehensive Test-Ban Treaty sometimes argue, that an end to US nuclear testing would stop proliferation, or testing by others. Surely Kim Jong II of North Korea, or President Ahmadinejad of Iran, or even the leaders of Pakistan and India, are relatively unimpressed by any American nuclear restraint. The first two tyrants are not easily inspired by acts of moral courage by other states.

India and Pakistan, for their part, tend to argue that a country like the United States with thousands of nuclear warheads in its inventory and almost a thousand nuclear tests under its belt is hardly in a position to deny others their nuclear rights. Any of these states, so goes the realist logic, will make nuclear-related decisions based much more on their own immediate security environments and agendas than out of concern for a global movement to limit the bomb's spread and lower its profile.

These are serious objections. They are probably correct to a large extent, at least for some overseas leaders much of the time. But they are not the end of the story or the argument.

A comprehensive test-ban treaty ... would help to reaffirm a norm, already acknowledged to a degree, that nuclear testing is unacceptable.

Sending a Strong Message

While regional security conditions do matter more than global arguments for most countries contemplating the bomb, a strong international message against proliferation can still affect their calculations. If there is a sense that 'everyone is doing it', leaders teetering on the edge of going nuclear will feel less restraint about doing so, and perhaps even an obligation to protect their own countries from the potential nuclear weapons of their neighbours. In this regard, maintaining a strong international dissuasive force against nuclearisation is important, for it affects perceptions of the likelihood of proliferation. Indeed, efforts to delegitimise the bomb over the past half century, and efforts to reduce testing and reduce arsenals over the last four decades, have helped convince governments in places such as South Korea, Japan, Taiwan, Argentina, Chile, Brazil, Saudi Arabia, Egypt and Germany not to pursue these weapons. Sometimes treaty critics will trivialise these accomplishments, noting, for example, that it would not be so bad if a country like Japan or Brazil got the bomb. But such arguments, even if correct, ignore the fact that once the 'nuclear tipping point', is crossed and momentum grows for getting the bomb around the world, it will not be just the Japans and Brazils that go nuclear.

Second, a comprehensive test-ban treaty would not physically prevent extremist states from getting the bomb, nor would it likely impress them with its moral force. But it would help reaffirm a norm, already acknowledged to a degree, that nuclear testing is unacceptable. This in turn will help discourage countries from testing the bomb out of fear that they will be punished if they do so. And if they test anyway, they will pay a price for it, which may convince them (or others) not to repeat the mistake. . . .

A comprehensive test-ban treaty will not physically prevent testing, of course. But combined with a renewed effort to allow and even assist civilian nuclear-power programmes, likely to grow in appeal in coming years with rising oil prices and concerns about global warming, it can shore up the international consensus about which types of nuclear activities are acceptable and which are not. A treaty should probably be complemented by even stronger support for the Additional Protocol (to improve monitoring of civilian nuclear programmes so that they are not easily transformed into military programmes) and creation of an international uranium fuel bank for civilian reactors (to discourage development of enrichment and reprocessing capabilities by most states). This new nuclear deal can help re-create a strong international consensus on nuclear policy. It will then be more feasible to apply serious punitive measures to any state that violates the rules, ideally deterring behaviour such as nuclear testing in the first place.

Is a Treaty Consistent with Stockpile Reliability?

Most agree that the United States needs a nuclear deterrent well into the foreseeable future. Common sense would seem to support the position that, at some point at least, testing will be needed to ensure the arsenal's reliability. How can one go 10, 20, 50 or 100 years without a single test and still be confident that the country's nuclear weapons will work? Equally importantly, how can one be sure that other countries will be deterred by an American stockpile that at some point will be certified only by the experiments and tests of a generation of physicists long since retired or dead?

From the nuclear-arms-control point of view, of course, some of this perception about the declining reliability of nuclear weapons might be welcomed. Declining reliability might translate into declining likelihood of the weapons ever being used and declining legitimacy for retention of a nuclear arsenal. At least, that could someday be the hope. But as a practical strategic and political matter, any test ban must still allow the United States to ensure 100% confidence in its nuclear deterrent into the indefinite future.

This should be possible without testing. To be sure, with time the reliability of a given warhead class may decline as its components age. In a worst case, it is conceivable that one category of warheads might in fact become flawed without our knowing it; indeed, this has happened in the past. But through a combination of monitoring, testing and remanufacturing the individual components, conducting sophisticated experiments (short of actual nuclear detonations) on integrated devices, and perhaps introducing a new warhead type or two of extremely conservative design into the inventory, the overall dependability of the American nuclear deterrent can remain very good. In other words, there might be a slight reduction in the overall technical capacities of the arsenal, but

93

still no question about its ability to exact a devastating response against anyone attacking the United States or its allies with nuclear or highly lethal biological weapons....

Might There Be New Needs for Nukes?

Some have suggested that a reason to preserve options for future nuclear testing lies in a potential need for new types of warheads to accomplish new missions. For example, in the 1980s, some missile-defence proponents were interested in a space-based nuclear-pumped X-ray laser. That was never particularly practical. But the idea of developing a nuclear weapon that could burrow underground *before* detonating has gained appeal, not least because countries such as North Korea and Iran are responding to America's increasingly precise conventional weaponry by hiding key weapons programmes well below the planet's surface.

One possible argument for such a warhead is to increase its overall destructive depth. In theory, the United States could modify the largest nuclear weapons in its stockpile to penetrate the ground. This approach would roughly double the destructive reach of the most powerful weapons in the current arsenal, according to physicist Michael Levi. But if an enemy can avoid weapons in the current arsenal, it could avoid the more powerful bombs by digging deeper underground. Given the quality of modern drilling equipment, that is not an onerous task.

A comprehensive test-ban treaty makes very good strategic sense for the United States and the world.

Earth-Penetrating Weapons

Could Earth-penetrating weapons at least reduce the nuclear fallout from an explosion? They could not prevent fallout; given limits on the hardness of materials and other basic physics, no useful nuclear weapon could penetrate the Earth far enough to keep the radioactive effects of its blast entirely below ground. But such weapons could reduce fallout. As a rule of thumb, it is possible to reduce the yield of a weapon tenfold (or more) while converting it into an Earth penetrator while maintaining the same destructive capability against underground targets that a normal weapon would have. This would reduce fallout by a factor of ten as well.

That would be a meaningful change. But is it really enough to change the basic usability of a nuclear device? Such a weapon would still produce a huge amount of fallout. Its use would still break the nuclear taboo. It would still only be capable of destroying underground targets if their locations were precisely known, in which case there is a good chance that conventional weapons or special forces could neutralise the target.

If such an Earth-penetrating weapon already existed, we might retain it for its marginal potential utility in a very rare class of possible scenarios. But the extremely limited set of circumstances for which it would have any utility at all means that it is hardly worth sacrificing a nuclear-testing moratorium, and the prospect of a comprehensive test ban, to develop such a capability. It is important to recall that, in the 1995 review of the Nuclear Non-Proliferation Treaty, ratification of the Comprehensive Test-Ban Treaty by the nuclear-weapons states was set forth by many non-nuclear states as a requirement if other countries were to sustain the tradition of non-proliferation.

The comprehensive test-ban treaty makes very good strategic sense for the United States and the world. The next American president should build on Bill Clinton's signing of that treaty, as well as George W. Bush's tacit compliance with its strictures, and send it to the US Senate for ratification. It makes sense whether Iran tests its own nuclear weapon in the coming years or not; either way, Washington will need more capacity to apply more pressure on states like Iran, and the treaty could help it garner international support for such pressure. American ratification of the treaty might also be part of a deal by which India and Pakistan agree not to do more testing themselves, joining the United States in a pledge of future nuclear-weapons restraint.

Organizations to Contact

The editors have compiled the following list of organizations concerned with the issues presented in this book. The descriptions are derived from materials provided by the organizations. The list was compiled on the date of publication of the present volume; the information provided here may change. Be aware that many organizations take several weeks or longer to respond to inquiries, so allow as much time as possible.

American Enterprise Institute (AEI)
1150 17th Street, NW, Washington, DC 20036
(202) 862-5800 • fax: (202) 862-7177
Web site: www.aei.org

AEI is a conservative think tank based in Washington, D.C. Its members support a strong and well-funded military and the use of force against rogue nations, particularly those that support terrorism or pursue nuclear weapons. AEI publishes books and the magazine *American Enterprise*, the current issue of which is available on its Web site. The AEI Web site also houses articles and commentary, including "Can a Nuclear Iran Be Contained or Deterred?" and "The End of Nuclear Diplomacy."

American Foreign Policy Council (AFPC)
1521 16th Street, NW, Washington, DC 20036
(202) 462-6055 • fax: (202) 462-6045
e-mail: afpc@afpc.org
Web site: www.afpc.org

Founded in 1982, the AFPC has as its goal to inform U.S. foreign policy and help world leaders build democracies and market economies. AFPC publishes bulletins on foreign policy issues, including the *Missile Defense Briefing Report*. On its

Web site, AFPC publishes links to articles concerning U.S. policy toward nations pursuing nuclear weapons, including "North Korea Wins Again" and "Why Tehran Wants the Bomb."

Arms Control Association (ACA)

1313 L Street, NW, Suite 130, Washington, DC   20005
(202) 463-8270 • fax: (202) 463-8273
e-mail: aca@armscontrol.org
Web site: www.armscontrol.org

Founded in 1971, ACA promotes public understanding of and support for effective arms control policies. It provides policy makers, the press, and the public with information, analysis, and commentary on arms control proposals, negotiations and agreements, and related national security issues. ACA publishes the monthly *Arms Control Today*, recent issues of which are available on its Web site. Archived articles available on its Web site include "Averting a Nonproliferation Disaster" and "Getting Real About Nuclear Disarmament."

Brookings Institution

1775 Massachusetts Avenue, NW, Washington, DC   20036
(202) 797-6000 • fax: (202) 797-6004
Web site: www.brookings.edu

Founded in 1927, the institution conducts research and analyzes global events and their impact on the United States and U.S. foreign policy. It publishes the quarterly *Brookings Review* and numerous books and research papers on foreign policy. Several reports on nuclear policy are available on the institution's Web site, including *Diplomatic Strategies for Dealing with Iran: How Tehran Might Respond* and *The Next Chapter: The United States and Pakistan.*

Cato Institute

1000 Massachusetts Avenue, NW
Washington, DC   20001-5403

(202) 842-0200 • fax: (202) 842-3490
Web site: www.cato.org

The institute is a libertarian public-policy research foundation dedicated to peace and limited government intervention in foreign affairs. It publishes numerous reports and periodicals, including *Policy Analysis* and *Cato Policy Review*, both of which discuss U.S. foreign policy options with nations that have or are believed to be pursing nuclear weapons. On its Web site, CATO members publish analysis and commentary on U.S. nuclear foreign policy, including "Iran's Nuclear Program: America's Policy Options" and "Nuclear Deterrence, Preventive War, and Counterproliferation."

Center for Strategic and International Studies (CSIS)
1800 K Street, NW, Washington, DC 20006
(202) 887-0200 • fax: (202) 775-3199
Web site: www.csis.org

CSIS is a public-policy research institution that specializes in U.S. domestic and foreign policy, national security, and economic policy. The center analyzes world crises and recommends U.S. military and defense policies. Its publications include the journal *Washington Quarterly*. The center also publishes numerous reports, including *Change and Challenge on the Korean Peninsula: Developments, Trends, and Issues* and *Combating Chemical, Biological, Radiological, and Nuclear Terrorism: A Comprehensive Strategy*.

Council on Foreign Relations
58 E. 68th Street, New York, NY 10021
(212) 434-9400 • fax: (212) 986-2984
Web site: www.cfr.org

The council specializes in foreign affairs and studies the international aspects of American political and economic policies. Its journal *Foreign Affairs*, published five times a year, includes analyses of U.S. foreign policy options with nations that have or are believed to be pursing nuclear weapons. Articles and commentary by CFR members are available on its Web site, including the report *A New National Security Strategy in an Age of Terrorists, Tyrants, and Weapons of Mass Destruction.*

Federation of American Scientists (FAS)

1717 K St., NW, Suite 209, Washington, DC   20036
(202) 546-3300 • fax: (202) 675-1010
Web site: www.fas.org

FAS was formed in 1945 by atomic scientists from the Manhattan Project who felt that scientists had an ethical obligation to bring their knowledge and experience to bear on critical national decisions, especially pertaining to nuclear weapons. Endorsed by 67 Nobel laureates in chemistry, economics, medicine, and physics, FAS promotes humanitarian uses of science and technology. It publishes the seasonal *Public Interest Report*, recent issues of which are available on its Web site. Also on the Web site is a Nuclear Information Project link, which includes information and analysis about the status and operations of nuclear weapons, the policies that guide their potential use, and developments in the nuclear fuel cycle.

Foreign Policy Association (FPA)

470 Park Avenue South, Second Floor, New York, NY   10016
(212) 481-8100 • fax: (212) 481-9275
e-mail: info@fpa.org
Web site: www.fpa.org

FPA is a nonprofit organization that believes a concerned and informed public is the foundation for effective foreign policy. Publications such as the annual *Great Decisions* briefing book and the quarterly *Headline Series* review U.S. foreign policy issues worldwide. FPA's *Global Q & A* series offers interviews with leading U.S. and foreign officials on issues concerning intelligence gathering, weapons of mass destruction, and military and diplomatic initiatives. Its Web site publishes articles and commentary on U.S. nuclear foreign policy, including "IAEA—a toothless Watchdog?" and "Nuclear Negotiations."

Global Security Institute (GSI)

GSB Building, Suite 400, One Belmont Avenue
Bala Cynwyd, PA   19004
(610) 668-5488 • fax: (610) 668-5489
e-mail: general@gsinstitute.org
Web site: www.gsinstitute.org

The goal of GSI is to strengthen international cooperation and security with a particular focus on nuclear arms control, nonproliferation, and disarmament. Founded by Senator Alan Cranston, the institute includes former heads of state and government, diplomats, politicians, celebrities, religious leaders, Nobel Peace laureates, disarmament and legal experts, and concerned citizens. On its Web site, GSI publishes policy briefs and briefing papers and recent issues of the periodic *PNND Notes*, a publication of its Parliamentarians for Nuclear Non-Proliferation and Disarmament program. Also on its Web site are links to previously published commentary on nuclear weapons issues, including "Sleepwalking in a Nuclear Minefield" and "Preventing Future Nuclear Catastrophes."

Heritage Foundation

214 Massachusetts Avenue, NE, Washington, DC   20002-4999
(800) 544-4843 • fax: (202) 544-6979
e-mail: pubs@heritage.org
Web site: www.heritage.org

The foundation is a public-policy research institute that advocates limited government and the free-market system. The foundation publishes the quarterly *Policy Review* as well as monographs, books, and papers supporting U.S. noninterventionism. Heritage publications on U.S. foreign policy include the *WebMemo* article "The Role of Nuclear Weapons in the 21st Century" and Heritage scholar testimony "U.S. Policy and Pakistan's Nuclear Weapons: Containing Threats and Encouraging Regional Security," which are available on its Web site. Other articles concerning U.S. nuclear weapons policy can be found through the Web site's search engine and on its Iran and Northeast Asia sections.

Nonproliferation Policy Education Center (NPEC)
1718 M Street, NW, Suite 244, Washington, DC   20036
(202) 466-4406 • fax: (202) 659-5429
Web site: www.npec-web.org

NPEC supports a robust nonproliferation policy. The center's goal is to promote a deeper understanding of multiple perspectives on proliferation. NPEC publishes the books *Pakistan's Nuclear Future: Worries Beyond War* and *Getting Ready for a Nuclear Ready Iran* and reports, some of which are available on its Web site, including *Evaluating America's Nonproliferation Bureaucracy*. The Web site also houses articles by NPEC staff, including "A Blink, a Nod, a Bomb" and "A World Provoked: Now How About We Do Something About Pyongyang?"

Nuclear Age Peace Foundation
1187 Coast Village Road, Suite 1, PMB 121
Santa Barbara, California   93108-2794
(805) 965-3443 • fax: (805) 568-466
Web site: www.wagingpeace.org

Founded in 1982, the Nuclear Age Peace Foundation, a nonprofit, nonpartisan international education and advocacy organization, initiates and supports worldwide efforts to abolish nuclear weapons, to strengthen international law and institutions, to use technology responsibly and sustainably, and to empower youth to create a more peaceful world. It publishes books such as *An Unacceptable Risk: Nuclear Weapons in a Volatile World* and the monthly e-newsletter *The Sunflower*, which provides news, information and analysis on nuclear and international security issues. Its Web site contains a searchable database of news, editorials, and articles, including "At the Nuclear Tipping Point" and "North Korean Nuclear Conflict Has Deep Roots."

Nuclear Threat Initiative (NTI)
1747 Pennsylvania Avenue, NW, Seventh Floor
Washington, DC   20006

(202) 296-4810 • fax: (202) 296-4811
e-mail: contact@nti.org
Web site: www.nti.org

NTI seeks to increase global security by reducing the risk from nuclear, biological, and chemical weapons and to build the trust, transparency, and security that are preconditions to the fulfillment of the Non-Proliferation Treaty's goals and ambitions. On its Web site, NTI publishes speeches, testimony, commentary, and analysis on nuclear weapons and proliferation, including "Securing the Bomb 2007," "Unite Against the Gravest Threat: Nuclear Terrorism," and "The Race Between Cooperation and Catastrophe."

Reason Foundation
3415 S. Sepulveda Boulevard, Suite 400
Los Angeles, CA 90034
(310) 391-2245 • fax: (310) 391-4395
Web site: www.reason.org

The foundation promotes individual freedoms and free-market principles, and it opposes U.S. interventionism in foreign affairs. Its publications include the monthly *Reason* magazine, recent issues of which are available at www.reason.com. The foundation Web site, linked to the Reason Public Policy Institute at www.rppi.org, publishes online versions of institute articles and reports, including "Learning to Love the Bomb: Is Nuclear Proliferation Inherently Dangerous?"

Union of Concerned Scientists (UCS)
2 Brattle Square, Cambridge, MA 02238-9105
(617) 547-5552 • fax: (617) 864-9405
Web site: www.ucsusa.org

UCS combines independent scientific research and citizen action to develop solutions and secure responsible changes in government policy, corporate practices, and consumer choices. Its scientists and policy experts work to reduce some of the biggest security threats facing the world today, including the risks posed by nuclear weapons. On its "Nuclear Weapons and Global Security" link, UCS publishes briefs, reports, and testimony on U.S. nuclear weapons policy, including "U.S. Nuclear Weapons Policy: Dangerous and Counterproductive" and "Disposition of Fissile Materials: Status and Prospects."

United Nations Association of the United States of America (UNA-USA)
801 Second Avenue, New York, NY   10017
(212) 907-1300 • fax: (212) 682-9185
e-mail: unahq@unausa.org
Web site: www.unausa.org

The association is a research organization whose goal is to strengthen the United Nations and U.S. participation in the council. Its publications include the quarterly newsmagazine the *InterDependent*, the biweekly *UNA-USA E-Newsletter*, the periodic *Washington Report*, and UNA-USA policy briefs. Recent issues of these publications are available on its Web site, including "The NPT at 35: A Crisis of Compliance or a Crisis of Confidence?"

U.S. Department of State, Bureau of International Security and Nonproliferation
2201 C Street, NW, Washington, DC   20520
(202) 647-4000
Web site: www.state.gov

The State Department is a federal agency that advises the president on the formulation and execution of foreign policy. One of the functions of the State Department's Bureau of International Security and Nonproliferation (ISN) is to administer policies to prevent the spread of weapons of mass destruction. Its section within the State Department's Web site includes information on nonproliferation programs, statements, and reports, including publications on nuclear terrorism.

Bibliography

Books

David Albright
and Corey
Hinderstein

*Dismantling the DPRK's Nuclear
Weapons Program: A Practicable,
Verifiable Plan of Action.* Washington,
DC: U.S. Institute of Peace, 2006.

Brian Alexander
and Alistair
Millar, eds.

*Tactical Nuclear Weapons: Emergent
Threats in an Evolving Security
Environment.* Washington, DC:
Brassey's, 2003.

Gawdat Bahgat

*Proliferation of Nuclear Weapons in
the Middle East.* Gainesville:
University Press of Florida, 2007.

Ian Bellany

*Curbing the Spread of Nuclear
Weapons.* Manchester, United
Kingdom: Manchester University
Press, 2005.

David J. Bishop

*Dismantling North Korea's Nuclear
Weapons Program.* Carlisle, PA:
Strategic Studies Institute, U.S. Army
War College, 2005.

Hans Blix

Why Nuclear Disarmament Matters.
Cambridge, MA: MIT Press, 2008.

Wyn Q. Bowen

*Libya and Nuclear Proliferation:
Stepping Back from the Brink.* New
York: Routledge for the International
Institute for Strategic Studies, 2006.

George Bunn and Christopher F. Chyba, eds.

U.S. Nuclear Weapons Policy: Confronting Today's Threats. Washington, DC: Brookings Institution Press, 2006.

Victor D. Cha and David C. Kang

Nuclear North Korea: A Debate on Engagement Strategies. New York: Columbia University Press, 2003.

Stephen J. Cimbala

Nuclear Weapons and Strategy: U.S. Nuclear Policy for the Twenty-First Century. New York: Routledge, 2005.

Lowell Dittmer, ed.

South Asia's Nuclear Security Dilemma: India, Pakistan, and China. Armonk, NY: L.M.E. Sharpe, 2005.

Daniel Doktori, ed.

Iran. New York: Columbia University Press, 2007.

Jacques L. Fuqua Jr.

Nuclear Endgame: The Need for Engagement with North Korea. Westport, CT: Praeger Security International, 2007.

Jacques E.C. Hymans

The Psychology of Nuclear Proliferation: Identity, Emotions, and Foreign Policy. New York: Cambridge University Press, 2006.

Michael I. Karpin

The Bomb in the Basement: How Israel Went Nuclear and What That Means for the World. New York: Simon and Schuster, 2006.

Suk Hi Kim and Semoon Chang, eds. *Economic Sanctions Against a Nuclear North Korea: An Analysis of United States and United Nations Actions Since 1950.* Jefferson, NC: McFarland, 2007.

Michel Korinman and John Laughland, eds. *Shia Power: Next Target Iran?* Portland, OR: Vallentine Mitchell Academic, 2007.

Morten Bremer Maerli and Sverre Lodgaard, eds. *Nuclear Proliferation and International Security.* New York: Routledge, 2007.

Michael E. O'Hanlon *Crisis on the Korean Peninsula: How to Deal with a Nuclear North Korea.* New York: McGraw-Hill, 2003.

Andrew O'Neil *Nuclear Proliferation in Northeast Asia: The Quest for Security.* New York: Palgrave Macmillan, 2007.

Arpit Rajain *Nuclear Deterrence in Southern Asia: China, India, and Pakistan.* Thousand Oaks, CA: Sage, 2005.

Gilbert Rozman *Strategic Thinking About the Korean Nuclear Crisis: Four Parties Caught Between North Korea and the United States.* New York: Palgrave Macmillan, 2007.

Scott D. Sagan and Kenneth N. Waltz *The Spread of Nuclear Weapons: A Debate Renewed.* New York: Norton, 2003.

James L. Schoff et al.   *Nuclear Matters in North Korea: Building a Multilateral Response for Future Stability in Northeast Asia.* Washington, DC: Potomac, 2008.

William C. Triplett   *Rogue State: How a Nuclear North Korea Threatens America.* Washington, DC: Regnery, 2004.

Periodicals

Graham Allison   "Deterring Kim Jong Il," *Washington Post*, October 27, 2006.

Graham Allison   "What About the Nukes? Despite Its Claims, Pakistan's Nuclear Weapons Are Vulnerable," *Newsweek*, December 28, 2007.

Bruce Bennett   "A New National Strategy for Korea: North Korea Threats Require Deterrence, Reconciliation," *Korea Herald*, March 13, 2008.

John R. Bolton   "Pyongyang's Upper Hand," *Wall Street Journal*, August 31, 2007.

Zev Chafets   "Israel Can Stand Up for Itself," *New York Times*, April 13, 2008.

Christianity Today   "Talk to Iran," July 9, 2008.

Steven Clemons   "Why Bush Won't Attack Iran," *Salon*, September 19, 2007.

Steve Coll   "The Fear That Terrorism Will Go Nuclear," *Sydney Morning Herald*, February 9, 2005.

Mary H. Cooper   "Nuclear Proliferation and
                      Terrorism," *CQ Researcher*, April 2,
                      2004.

Ivo H. Daalder   "Nuclear Weapons in the Age of
and Jeffrey Lewis   al-Qaeda," *Financial Times*, August
                      13, 2007.

Economist   "It's Later Than You Think," June 26,
                      2008.

Federation of   *Toward True Security: Ten Steps the*
American   *Next President Should Take to*
Scientists, Natural   *Transform U.S. Nuclear Weapons*
Resources Defense   *Policy*, February 2008.
Council, and   http://docs.nrdc.org/nuclear/files/
Union of   nuc_08021201A.pdf.
Concerned
Scientists

Michael J. Gerson   "In North Korea, Process over
                      Progress," *Washington Post*, February
                      1, 2008.

Peter Grier   "Could North Korea Still Make
                      Nukes?" *Christian Science Monitor*,
                      July 2, 2008.

Seymour M.   "The Iran Plans," *New Yorker*, April
Hersh   17, 2006.

Brian Michael   "Nuclear Terror: How Real?"
Jenkins   *Washington Times*, May 13, 2007.

Max M.   "We Should, So We Can: Life
Kampelman   Without the Bomb," *International
                      Herald Tribune*, April 25, 2006.

Peter Katel   "U.S. Policy on Iran," *CQ Researcher*, November 16, 2007.

Charles Krauthammer   "Deterring the Undeterrable," *Washington Post*, April 18, 2008.

William Langewiesche   "How to Get a Nuclear Bomb," *Atlantic Monthly*, December 2006.

Andrei Lankov   "Staying Alive: Why North Korea Will Not Change," *Foreign Affairs*, March–April 2008.

Winston Lord and Leslie H. Gelb   "Yielding to N. Korea Too Often," *Washington Post*, April 26, 2008.

Los Angeles Times   "Iran's Nonexistent Nuclear Program," December 5, 2007.

Rod Lyon   "Deterrence the Name of the Game," *Australian*, July 7, 2008.

Physicians for Social Responsibility   *War Is Not the Answer*, March 2007. www.psr.org/site/DocServer/ WarIsNotTheAnswer.pdf?docID=2181.

Bennett Ramberg   "The Right Way to Keep Tabs on Iran's Nuclear Program," *Christian Science Monitor*, December 6, 2007.

Jeffrey Record   "Nuclear Deterrence, Preventive War, and Counterproliferation," *CATO Policy Analysis*, July 8, 2004.

Tilman Ruff   "Let's Ban All Nuclear Weapons—Now," *The Age [Australia]*, October 28, 2007.

Claude Salhani   "Will Terrorists Go Nuclear?" *United Press International*, July 7, 2008.

Amir Taheri   "Bombs Away," *New York Post*, June 15, 2008.

Siddharth   "The Nuclear Deal and 'Minimum
Varadarajan   Deterrence,'" *The Hindu*, October 7, 2006.

Stephen Zunes   "Arms Transfers to Pakistan Undermine U.S. Foreign Policy Goals," *National Catholic Reporter*, May 20, 2005.

Index